D0221277

RIVERS IN WORLD HISTORY

THE VOLGA RIVER

Tim McNeese

CHELSEA HOUSE
PUBLISHERS
A Haights Cross Communications ✦ Company ®
Philadelphia

FRONTIS: A satellite image of the Volga River emptying into the Caspian Sea. The Volga, Europe's longest river, begins its nearly 2,300-mile trek just to the northwest of Moscow and flows past such Russian cities as Volgograd (formerly Stalingrad), Nizhny Novgorod, and Samara on its way to the Caspian.

CHELSEA HOUSE PUBLISHERS

VP, NEW PRODUCT DEVELOPMENT Sally Cheney
DIRECTOR OF PRODUCTION Kim Shinners
CREATIVE MANAGER Takeshi Takahashi
MANUFACTURING MANAGER Diann Grasse

Staff for THE VOLGA RIVER

EXECUTIVE EDITOR Lee Marcott
EDITOR Christian Green
PRODUCTION EDITOR Noelle Nardone
PHOTO EDITOR Sarah Bloom
SERIES AND COVER DESIGNER Keith Trego
LAYOUT 21st Century Publishing and Communications, Inc.

A Haights Cross Communications Company ®

First Printing

9 8 7 6 5 4 3 2 1

Library of Congress Cataloging-in-Publication Data

McNeese, Tim.
   The Volga river/Tim McNeese.
      p. cm.—(Rivers in world history)
   Includes bibliographical references.
   ISBN 0-7910-8247-4 (cloth)
  1. Volga River Region (Russia)—History. I. Title. II. Series.
DK511.V65M36 2005
947'.4—dc22
                                                        2004022017

All links and Web addresses were checked and verified to be correct at the time of publication. Because of the dynamic nature of the Web, some addresses and links may have changed since publication and may no longer be valid.

CONTENTS

1

A Nation's Great River

Today's Russian people, the modern-day descendants of countless tribes of nomads, traders, and invaders, call their great river—a seemingly endless stream that embodies the lifeblood of Russia's history and inhabitants—"Mother Volga." Some of their ancestors had their own names for the grand, flowing Eurasian river. The ancient Greeks called it the Ra. To the medieval Tatars, it was the Itil. The Volga has been such an important river throughout history that it has also been called "the cradle of Russia."

At 2,300 miles, the Volga is the longest river in Europe, and it has been witness to much of Russia's history. Through the centuries, this immense, snaking Eurasian waterway has served as a thoroughfare of transportation, commerce, and, in more recent years, tourism. Its drainage basin is immense, spreading across two-fifths of the European half of modern Russia, where half of the population of the Russian Republic lives.

The Volga's origins are nestled in the Valdai Hills, which are northwest of Moscow, the Russian capital. Along its course, the Volga's elevation drops slowly from its source at 750 feet above sea level to its Caspian Sea mouth at 92 feet below sea level. Along the way from Valdai to the Caspian, the waters of the Volga are fed by 200 tributary rivers, most of which flow in along the main river's left bank. Combining the main tributaries with more than 150,000 additional rivers and streams, the Volga watershed includes more than 330,000 miles of waterway, draining more than 500,000 square miles from the Central Russian Upland in the west to Saratov in the south.

Today, nearly all of the Volga is navigable, largely because of the building of dams that control the river's flow in an arcing, southern direction until it empties into the Caspian Sea. Many of the water impoundment facilities, which include nine hydroelectric power stations, provide electricity for Russian cities.

The people of Russia have gathered to engage in economic activity everywhere along the river: Approximately 50 percent

The Volga rises out of the Valdai Hills, an area with an abundance of glacial lakes, and flows east past the towns of Yaroslavl and Nizhny Novgorod. The Volga has 200 tributary rivers and approximately 40 percent of Russians live near the Volga's watershed.

of Russian industry is situated on the Volga or its tributaries. The Volga carries two-thirds of all Russian freight cargo, which includes a large amount of natural resources from the vast Russian interior. One of every four cargo vessels on the Volga carries timber and raw wood products. Additional major cargoes include oil and other petroleum products, coal, foodstuffs, salt, tractors, cars and trucks, and chemicals and fertilizers. Such freighters are able to navigate approximately 2,000 of the Volga's 2,300 miles, and about 70 of the river's 200 main tributaries are also navigable by cargo ships.

Two of every five Russians live in close proximity to the Volga's watershed. Nearly half of the Russians who take passage on their country's inland waterways ply the Volga and its many tributaries. Half of the country's farmers live on or near the Volga, where many raise abundant fields of wheat in the river's fertile bottomlands.

To encourage the expansion and viability of trade along the Volga, the Russians have constructed several man-made waterways that join the river's waters. The Volga-Baltic Waterway delivers the Volga to the Baltic Sea. From there, the White Sea–Baltic Canal connects the Baltic with the White Sea. The Moscow Canal links the Russian capital directly to the Volga, and the Volga reaches the Don River, as well as the Sea of Azov via the Volga-Don Ship Canal.

The course of the Volga River is typically divided into three topographical regions, identified as the Upper, Middle, and Lower Volga. The Upper Volga stretches from its source to its confluence with the Oka River. The Middle Volga runs from the Oka confluence to its juncture with the Kama River. The third region of the river spans its final length from the Kama confluence to the Caspian Sea.

Each region of the river is unique. At its origin, the Volga is a small waterway—more stream than river—as it flows across the Valdai Hills. It becomes a river only after it has been joined by several of its tributaries. The Upper Volga reaches several small lakes and then takes on water from the Selizharovka River. As it flows on, the Volga moves to the southeast along a terraced trench and then passes the town of Rzhev, where its course turns to the northeast. Its waters are increased by the inflow of the Vazuza and Tvertsa Rivers near the town of Tver (formerly Kalinin). Holding steady to the northeast, the Volga reaches the Rybinsk Reservoir, which contains the water of other rivers, including the Mologa and Sheksna. The Volga flows out of the Rybinsk to the southeast, along a narrow valley hidden by heavy forest between the Uglich Highlands to the south and the Danilov Upland and Galich-Chukhlom Lowland to the north. Downstream, the Volga flows past additional lowlands, where tributaries including the Kostroma, Unzha, and Oka Rivers flow into the main river course.

Here, the middle leg of the Volga begins. Flowing east-southeast from the Oka confluence to the city of Kazan, the waters of the Volga swell, increasing in volume by 100 percent. More tributaries, including the Sura and Sviyaga Rivers, reach the great Russian river from the right, and the Kerzhenets and Vetluga join the Volga along its left bank. Near Kazan, the Volga veers to the south and reaches the Samara Reservoir, where its greatest tributary, the Kama River, adds its immense flow.

South of the Kama confluence, the Volga moves into its lower region, becoming a river of great dimension. For the most part, the river flows southwest in this region, gliding along the base of the Volga Hills straight toward one of its greatest cities, Volgograd, formerly Stalingrad, which faced a massive siege from the German Wehrmacht (war machine) during World War II. Most of the rivers that join the Volga along this stretch, including the Samara, Bolshoy Irgiz, and Yeruslan, are small and reach the river along its left bank.

One river leaves the Volga along this stretch. Just upriver from Volgograd, the Volga's main distributary river, the Akhtuba, branches to the southeast and finally reaches the Caspian Sea independently of the main river. As the Volga turns to the southeast in this same region, it is often paralleled by the Akhtuba. Between the two rivers, the region is a floodplain marked by interconnected channels and cutoffs. As the Volga passes through this lowland region, a second distributary river, the Buzan, splits off just upriver from the city of Astrakhan. This area marks the expansion of the Volga's delta region, a vast watery territory that covers more than 7,300 square miles—the largest delta in Russia. In addition to the Buzan and Akhtuba Rivers, the Volga Delta includes the Bakhtemir, Kamyzyak, Staraya (Old) Volga, and Bolda Rivers.

The waters drained by the Volga and its tributaries are as extensive as the great river itself. The majority of the Volga's water (60 percent of its annual discharge) comes from snowfall in the higher elevations. An additional 30 percent comes from underground springs and other subterranean water sources. Rainfall accounts for the remaining 10 percent. Much of the volume and flow of the Volga today is regulated artificially by the multiple dam systems on the river. Flooding remains common on the portions of the river that are unharnessed; where the Volga is still an unruly waterway and spring floods (*polovodye* in Russian) are as much a problem today as at any other time in the river's history. Before the dam system was built on the Volga, the river's water level might vary from 23 to 36 feet on the Upper Volga, 39 to 46 feet on the Middle Volga, and from 10 to nearly 50 feet on the lower reaches.

Fed by many peripheral streams and confluent rivers, the Volga adds to its overall water flow as it continues toward the Caspian. Along the river's upper stages, the Volga's flow might be less than 7,000 cubic feet per second. Less than 200 miles downstream, at the city of Yaroslavl, the river's volume dramatically increases to 40,000 cubic feet per second. These amounts are dwarfed when compared to the amount of water that passes along the river at Samara, in the Middle Volga, where water rushes along at 270,000 cubic feet per second. At the river's mouth, the water amount runs even higher, even though the Volga loses 2 percent of its flow to evaporation.

With such great length, the river passes through several climates from north to south. From the Volga's source through

The Kama River, the Volga's largest tributary, serves as the southern boundary of the stretch of river known as the Middle Volga. Here, the Trans-Siberian Railroad crosses the Kama River near Perm, which is east of the Volga, in the Ural Mountain region of Russia.

its middle course, the climate of the river's basin is a temperate zone marked alternately by frigid, snowy winters and warm, humid summers. Below Kama (the southern end of the Middle Volga) to the Volga Hills, the river passes through a climate region that includes hot, dry summers and cold wintry weather, but with much less snow. Along the Volga's southern length, there is less rain and the climate is hotter during the summer, which is the source of much of the Lower Volga's evaporation loss. Here, the annual rainfall is typically half that along the Upper Volga (25 inches versus 12 inches).

Despite the differences in climate along the Volga, the river freezes along its entire length in winter. The Upper and Middle Volga sections generally begin to freeze by the end of November, and the Lower Volga freezes a few weeks later, in December. With the passing of a typical bitter cold winter, the great river experiences the thaw delivered by a warm Russian spring. Near Astrakhan, the ice breakup begins by mid-March, at Kamyshin by early April, and everywhere else by mid-April. Despite the legendary cold of Russian winters, the entire Volga generally is free of ice for approximately 200 days annually and, near Astrakhan, for two additional months.

Much of Russian history is centered in the region of the Eurasian plain, a broad expanse of ground that covers approximately 9 million square miles, "the largest extent of land on the earth's surface."[1] This vast world of difficult terrain, one marked by numerous rivers and streams, including the mighty Volga, has been occupied for thousands of years by a divergent mixture of peoples and cultures. Despite the extreme climate and terrain, the Eurasain plain has been home to people for thousands of years.

Approximately 15,000 years ago, at the end of the most recent ice age, glaciers covered much of the region of northern Europe, including the modern-day Volga River and its neighboring rivers and tributaries. As the glaciers began to recede, green belts —regions where vegetation could survive and even thrive— began to develop. North of the Arctic Circle, this vegetation was little more than mosses and lichens. South of the tundra, the topographic-climatic region of the taiga developed. This is a portion of northern Europe that includes "a vast belt of dense coniferous forests, broken only by peat bogs, which extends from Finland eastward for four thousand miles to the Bering Sea."[2] In this more hospitable region, amazing numbers of fur-bearing animals—everything from squirrels and ermine to sable, foxes, and bears—came to live. Early prehistoric peoples caught these animals for survival, and later hunters and trappers built an economic empire on a lucrative fur trade and helped establish early Russia.

Throughout the taiga, great spreads of birch, fir, and pine trees developed; largely centered in a giant geographic triangle running from the Baltic Sea to the east toward modern-day Poland and narrowing in the vicinity of the Ural Mountains. The inhospitable soils of this region supported little tree growth, but another geographic factor was eventually responsible for helping to bring millions of residents into the Russian region: Across these lands, the retreating glaciers of the Ice Age carved out the courses of dozens of important Russian rivers, including the Dnieper, Dniester, Don, Dvina, and the longest of them all—the Volga.

2

Early People
of the Volga

For thousands of years, the lands of Russia have been occupied by a varied succession of inhabitants whose diversity has added to Russia's cultural make up. This multicultural mixture includes a variety of Asian and European peoples, as well as others from the ancient Near East and beyond. Anthropologists do not agree on when the first inhabitants reached the Russian steppes and its rivers, including the Volga, but it is clear that, about 5,000 years ago, Indo-European peoples living in the Russian forests had a social system in place and were hunting and fishing to survive. Their society was primitive, but through successive centuries, it developed to include systematic agriculture and animal domestication.

The peoples living along the steppes of Russia were also creating social systems. Here, around 3000 B.C., the region of the Volga was becoming permanently occupied as village life encouraged less nomadism and a more sedentary existence. Within a millennium, during the Bronze Age (2000–1000 B.C.), those living along the steppes were developing a more complicated lifestyle than their neighbors in the forests to the north. These early occupants of the Volga region relied more on farming and raising cattle than ever before.

Who exactly were these early, Neolithic peoples? This is a complicated question with no clear answers. It appears to anthropologists that each culture group lived within its own sphere of influence alongside other tribal and cultural groups, with none dominating the others. They used the Volga and other rivers as highways, during both summer and winter months. In winter, they "took repeated advantage of the frozen rivers as ready-made roads by which to penetrate into the depths of the forests." [3]

Then, around 1000 B.C., an Aryan group of nomads called the Cimmerians began to conquer their neighbors throughout the central region of Russia and along the Lower Volga. Little is known about these aggressive peoples. They came to rule the southern region of Russia and the Volga for three centuries, from approximately 1000 to 700 B.C., and their influence spread deep into the Caucasus region. (For additional information on these early inhabitants of the Lower Volga region, enter "Cimmerians" into any search engine and browse the many sites listed.)

THE SCYTHIANS

The centuries of Cimmerian dominance in central Russia came to an end around 700 B.C. with the rise of the Scythians. Information about where the Scythians came from is incomplete, although it is known that they arrived along the banks of the Volga from the east. The Scythians became the first of several streams of invaders to reach the Volga region and establish themselves as the arbiters of power. They had crossed Asia through Turkistan along a primary horse road south of the Ural Mountains. Others followed during the next half millennium.

What made them leave their homelands in Asia to settle west of the Volga is uncertain. Such major cultural and geographic shifts are often preceded by drought, a growing population that exhausts resources, or pressure exerted by other cultural groups that push their neighbors off their lands. Like a giant game of falling dominoes, the aggression of one group leads another, such as the Scythians, to menace those west of them. History records the Scythians as a people bound to the horse and known for their courage, fortitude, and savagery in battle. Their numbers included pastoralists who herded cattle, goats, and sheep. These domesticated animals were in constant need of new grasslands, causing the Scythians to always remain in search of new lands for grazing. As the Scythians moved, they carried their household items in felt-covered wagons pulled by oxen; these wagons also provided them with mobile shelter and sleeping space. As nomads, they often ate on the run, with meat and

The Scythians, who migrated to the Volga River region from central Asia between 800 and 600 B.C., were a nomadic tribe known for their skilled archers and horsemanship. This fourth century B.C. Scythian sword is displayed at Kiev's Historical Treasures Museum, which is renowned for its collection of Scythian goldwork.

a drink called *kumiss,* which was fermented mare's milk, serving as the mainstay of their diet.

In battle, the Scythians were a formidable enemy. They were bred in the saddle and were capable of riding long distances during military campaigns and raids. Their horsemanship allowed them to use hit-and-run tactics against their enemies. According to the writings of the famous Greek historian and travel writer Herodotus, the Scythians ran rings around a sixth-century B.C. Persian force with their superior equestrian skills: "They resolved, as the neighboring nations refused their alliance, that they would not openly venture on any pitched battle with the enemy, but would retire before them, driving off their herds, choking up all the wells and springs as they retreated, and leaving the whole country bare of forage."[4] In his endless personal travels, Herodotus also noted that the Scythians were "more unpolished than those of any other region that we know of."[5]

They were able to embarrass an enemy without meeting them in battle, but the Scythians were capable fighters. The popular Scythian weapon was a short, "double-curved" bow, with which battlers fired bronze-tipped arrows with great accuracy for nearly the length of a football field. When they conquered an enemy's village, they took prisoners and made them slaves. Sometimes, they allowed a conquered tribe or village to remain intact, but their victims were forced to accept Scythian rule and were required to pay tribute to their conquerors.

During the centuries of Scythian dominance in the Volga region, the Greeks were extending their power far beyond their home waters of the Mediterranean Sea. When the Greeks reached the shores of the Black Sea, they established a trade system with the Scythians. The Scythians bartered grain, fish, and amber to Greek traders in exchange for Aegean wines, olive oil, textiles and cloth goods, and luxury items.

THE SARMATIANS

The days of Scythian dominance came to an end around 200 B.C. with the arrival of the Sarmatians, an Iranian people who came from central Asia and whose control of the Volga region lasted for four centuries. Although the Scythians and the Sarmatians were similar culturally, there were important differences that allowed the Sarmatians to conquer the Scythians. The Sarmatians "used stirrups and armor, lances, and long swords in contrast to the light equipment of the Scythians."[6] The Sarmatians were also able to adapt quickly to life in southern Russia and so did not have to experience a prolonged period of adjustment to their new home. They also managed to keep the major trade route that ran across southern Russia and connected Asia with Europe open.

The Sarmatians consisted of several different tribes, some more dominant than others. Among the most powerful and influential were the Alans, in part because of their superior numbers among their Sarmatian brethren. Contemporaries described the Alans as "tall and blond, excelling in horsemanship and in metalwork."[7] In modern Russia, the descendents of the Alans are known as the Ossetians; they live in southern Russia. According to some historians, the ethnic term "Rus" or "Rhos," which is sometimes credited as the source for the word *Russia* (though Western historians believe it comes from the Vikings), refers to a clan of the Alan tribe, the *Rukhs-As*, or the "Light Alans."

THE VÖLKERWANDERUNG

Sarmatian dominance over peoples throughout central Asia and the Volga region lasted from the late decades of the third century B.C. until the early decades of the third century A.D. During those centuries, the Italic peoples known as the Romans had extended their dominance throughout the Mediterranean at the expense of the Greeks and many others. By the third and fourth century A.D., the vast Roman Empire, by then corrupt, decentralized, and decaying from within, was beginning to experience outside pressure exerted by restless Germanic barbarians to the north. As these Germanic tribesmen began to menace the Romans, their *Völkerwanderung,* "peoples' journey," also changed life for the Sarmatians and those living in the Volga region.

Invasions reached the region of the Volga from both the west and the east. A Germanic tribe known as the Goths reached southern Russia after being turned out of southern Europe by the Romans. Once they reached the Volga and its surrounding countryside in the late third century, the Goths began to adapt to their new world. Astonishingly, the Goths had migrated from the Baltic region to the Black Sea on foot. Not natural horsemen, the Goths had to develop their ability to fight while on horseback, a prerequisite to defeating new enemies, such as the Sarmatians, along the steppes. They also became adept at sea travel and sailed their ships along the "shores of the Black Sea and even of the Aegean, attacking Athens in 267 A.D."[8] The Goths did not remain in control of the Volga and southern Russia for long, because they soon faced invasions from another enemy—this one arriving in the Volga region from the east: the Huns.

THE HUNS

These Asiatic horsemen were busy invading to the west across much of eastern Europe during the fourth century. They reached the Russian steppes around A.D. 370 and drove the Goths back toward the borders of the Roman Empire. The Huns quickly established an extensive European power base "extending from the Volga to the Danube."[9] In the meantime, two tribal groups of Goths—the Visigoths (the West Goths) and the Ostrogoths (the East Goths)—secured permission from the Romans to enter the empire west of the Danube River to escape the ferocity of these violent Asian invaders. Many of the Alans added their frightened numbers to the retreating Goths.

The Russian and European empire of the Huns reached its high point during the time of leadership provided by their greatest military leader, Attila (c. 406–453). Known in history as the "Scourge of God," Attila and his troops terrorized the region of the Volga and farther west, and succeeded in establishing military headquarters on the plains of Hungary. From there, they forced the once-mighty Roman Empire as well as the New Rome, Constantinople, to pay them tribute. The reign of power wielded by the Huns did not last long, however. Just as Attila was preparing to advance farther across Europe, intent

The Huns entered the Russian steppes in the late fourth century A.D., where they established a power base that extended from the Volga River in the east to the Danube River in the west. Attila the Hun, known as the "Scourge of God" for his cruelty and barbarism, was the most powerful leader of this nomadic tribe who originated in Mongolia.

on taking control of the entire continent, he died suddenly, the victim of a prolonged and fatal nosebleed on the night of one of his political marriages.

THE AVARS

In the wake of the once-powerful Huns, another group of Asiatic nomad invaders, the Bulgars, ruled for a short time, only to be overtaken by the Avars during the mid-sixth century. They were yet another "Asiatic, Mongol- and Turkic-speaking"[10] invading tribe and they became "the most dreaded military force of their time."[11] Although they did not succeed in capturing as large an empire across Russia as had the Huns, their lands reached from the Volga to the Elbe River. The Avar state was smaller than its predecessor, but it lasted longer—a century on Russian soil and more than 250 years elsewhere. During their zenith of power, the Avars ruled Russia from the Volga to the Danubian Plain. From this central European locale, the Avars were able to challenge East Rome, the empire of the Byzantines (the Roman Empire had finally collapsed during the late fifth century), and even went to war with Emperor Charlemagne, the king of the Franks, during the late eighth century.

THE KHAZARS

The Avars were not without their challengers. During the seventh century, another invading military culture forced itself into southern Russia, directly along the Lower Volga, and swept north to the Caucasus and onto the Russian steppes to the east. These wide-ranging invaders were the Khazars. They traced their roots from the old Hunnish Bulgars and Altaic Turks, those who had fought with the Avars in the sixth century. By the eighth century, the Khazars were ruling over the lands lying between the great Russian rivers, including the Volga, Don, Dnieper, and Dniester. They maintained a close alliance to the Byzantines ruling from Constantinople, whom they helped in their conflict with the Persians. When Muslim armies rode hard from Arabia into southern Russia, the Khazars met them in battle and experienced crushing defeats. Still, they ultimately managed to turn the tide of Islam's expansion into Russia.

The Khazars refused to convert to Christianity, although they traded and allied themselves extensively with the Christian emperors who ruled Constantinople and the Byzantine Empire. During the eighth or ninth century, the rulers of the Khazars converted to Judaism after giving sanctuary to Jews who had been driven out of Constantinople. The majority of the Khazar population did not take up the Jewish faith, but religious freedom was an important part of the Khazar state, as "pagans, Moslems, Christians, and Jews mingled in Khazaria, where all enjoyed considerable freedom and autonomy to live under their own laws." [12]

The Volga served as a centerpiece for the Khazar Empire. Its capital, Itil, was situated along the banks of the Volga River, near its mouth. This settlement "developed from a winter city of skin tents into a great commercial town." [13] Itil became a vital link in the trade with the Byzantines, and its streets featured a wide array of market shops and open-air trading centers. The Khazars also established other important settlement cities, such as Samandar. Trade flourished throughout the Khazar kingdom, providing the backbone of its power. As one historian has explained, "The prosperity of Khazaria evidently depended less on the resources of the country than on its favorable position across important trade-routes." [14]

During the ninth century, the Khazars were challenged by invading Turkish forces known as the Pechenegs (or Patzinaks). The Khazar emperor established another important town, Sarkel, on the Don River, where he ordered the construction of the first stone fortress in the Steppe region. The Khazars did succeed in turning back the Pecheneg advance and ousting this group from the lands between the Volga and the Urals to the north. The Pecheneg threat did not completely disappear, however. Driven to the west, they pushed the Magyars, who had been ruled by the Khazars, farther west, beyond the Carpathian Mountains, into modern-day Hungary, where the Avars had formerly ruled. Here, the Magyars established the kingdom of Hungary. The Pechenegs settled along the Lower Dnieper River and continued to harass their surrounding neighbors.

THE LAND OF THE EAST SLAVS

For centuries, a seemingly endless number of foreign invaders managed to find their way to the region of the Volga and South-Central Russia. The Scythians, the Huns, the Avars, the Bulgars, and the Magyars all experienced a time of ascendancy and control over Russian territory. Others—including the Cumans, Mongols, Turks, and Tatars—came later, until foreigners had been invading the Volga region for more than 1,000 years. As one historian summed up this recurring pattern of invasion, control, and disintegration: "The steppe lands of southern Russia were like a great highway along which nomadic hordes fought for dominion and for the rich trade between China and Europe, only to be crushed or pushed farther to the west by a new tribe."[15] Even as this revolving drama of repeated conquests unfolded, yet another group of invaders reached the great plains along the Volga and beyond—the Slavs.

Where these nomadic peoples first emerged is unknown. They were known to the Romans as early as the first century A.D., and the great Roman writer and historian Tacitus recorded these tribes as the Veneti, Antes, or the Wends, who had already settled along the Vistula River basin and in the region of the Upper Dnieper, in the modern-day lands of Poland and Belarus. Tacitus noted that the Slavs were in a state of expansion, spreading to the west toward the Carpathian Mountains and to east of the Danube, as well as northeast into the Russian forest regions. During the following centuries of migratory development, the Slavic tribes branched into three distinct ethnic groups, including the West Slavs, who had settled along the Vistula River and whose modern descendents are the Poles and Czechs; the

South Slavs, who reached the Balkans, in such modern-day states as Kosovo, Albania, Montenegro, and Bosnia; and the East Slavs, who would eventually split into further fractured tribal units called *ulus*. Many of these peoples, including the Derevlians, Dregovichians, Dulebians, Krivichians, Polotians, Radimichians, Severians, Slovenes, Tivercians, Ulichians, Volhynians, and Vyatichians, became the ancestors of modern Russians.

Once they migrated into modern-day Russia, many of these Slavic peoples chose to live in the dark, heavy forest-lands at a distance from the horsebound nomads of the steppes. The Slavs migrated along the natural river routes, in part to make trade connections with neighboring tribesmen, including the Khazars. In the early years after the Slavs' arrival in southern Russia, they paid tribute to the Khazars, but, over time, they became involved more directly in the region's extensive trade systems, "sending goods and slaves, mainly the fair-haired Finns so much in demand in the slave markets of the Mediterranean." [16] The Slavs engaged not only in regional trade but also in regional war. Historians record that the East Slavs battled with the Goths and the Huns, who pushed to the west.

As the East Slavic presence in Russia developed, these people formed permanent settlements and complicated economic systems. By the 800s, their agricultural practices were well established. They were also adept at fishing, hunting, and cattle raising. Their craft skills included weaving and pottery, as well as woodworking. They were also skilled in iron making. The East Slavs of the ninth century established hundreds of towns and villages; some of their most important urban settlements included Novgorod, Smolensk, and Kiev, a town that would become one of the most important in Russian history.

By the 1100s, the East Slavs were divided into a dozen tribal groups that lived along the great Russian plains region, which stretched from "the Black Sea, the Danube, and the Carpathian mountains, across the Ukraine, and beyond, northward to the Novgorod territory and eastward toward the Volga."[17] By that time, they were facing yet another group of nomadic invaders: Scandinavians, who were settling up and down the easily accessible interior waterways of the Volga and other Russian rivers. The invasions of these ruddy, bearded warriors from the frigid lands of northern Europe would forever change the history of Russia and the Volga River.

The Rus

D uring the ninth century, the wide-ranging mix of peoples living along the Volga and its tributaries were forced to make room for a new ethnic group, one that reached the lands of western Russia by using those same rivers. They were referred to by various names over the following centuries as they made contact, often violently, with nearly every culture living in Europe, from the farthest coastlands of Ireland to the warm waters of the Mediterranean to the Volga itself. To the Slavs who had entered the Volga region two centuries earlier, these intimidating, seafaring invaders were known as the Varangians. To others they were the Rus or Rhos, an identity perhaps derived from the Finnish word for "rowers" and the source for the later geographic term *Russia*. They were Norsemen who reached the Volga region from their homelands in Scandinavia but are more commonly known today as Vikings—a name that conjures up both images of terrifying raids and looting, and a great era of exploration and discovery as far west as North America.

The Varangians of the ninth century were generally sea-going adventurers of Danish and Swedish origin. They were to become legendary over the next three centuries for their highly skilled seamanship and violent acts of warfare. They became infamous for their constant raiding and pillaging of European towns, seaports, and monasteries. From the eighth century until the eleventh century, such Norsemen were spreading out in every direction. Their adventures sent them to the four corners of the known world, to such remote locales as Baghdad and Constantinople and perhaps as far east as China. They might have been the first Europeans to reach the Western Hemisphere: Their sagas weave narratives of sailing and island-hopping from their Scandinavian homelands to Iceland, then to Greenland, across the North Atlantic to modern-day Canada, and even as far south as what is now the state of Maryland. Through their constant restless migrations and explorations, they founded numerous colonies and trading stations, including several along the Volga River. Their shallow-draft ships, some specially designed for river travel and carved out of a single tree trunk, traversed the Lovat, Dnieper, Donets, and Don Rivers to reach the Black Sea, and they relied on the Northern Dvina and the Volga to deliver them to the Caspian Sea region.

As the Vikings spread their influence far and wide, they often raided and took control of established towns, putting down any resistance with great violence. For many, the Viking warrior was greatly feared. Norsemen were trained to fight from a young age, and they seemed to be fearless. They carried several weapons, including spears, swords, axes and hatchets, and a variety of knives and daggers, into battle. Some Viking warriors were known as berserks, who fought naked except for a "bear shirt" or wolf skin. Such ferocious warriors "howled and bit their shields and fought with a snarling rage."[18]

THE VIKINGS REACH THE VOLGA

Historic tradition places the year A.D. 862 as the date for the first documented Viking raids in Russia. That year, a Varangian prince named Rurik reached the Slavic settlement of Novgorod. Perhaps the only significant source for this bit of Viking history is a document called the *Primary Chronicle*, which was based on oral tradition and set down by monks two centuries later. The accuracy of the document's details remains controversial. According to the *Primary Chronicle*, the Slavs of Novgorod had rebelled against earlier Varangian colonization only to reinvite the Vikings back when rival factions of Slavs "threatened to reduce the city and its extensive trade to chaos."[19] The Danish feudal lord Rurik entered Novgorod in the company of two fellow warriors, Askold and Dir, who may have been his brothers—or may have been only legends. These

Rurik, a Varangian (Viking) warrior, gained control of the Slavic town of Novgorod in 862 and ruled until his death in 879. Rurik's successor, Oleg, formally set up the Kievan Rus—the precursor to the Russian state—and his line of succession lasted through Fedor I, who died in 1598.

two did not remain in Novgorod, choosing instead to establish their rule over other Slavic peoples. They ventured 600 miles south to Kiev, where they founded the state that would be the origins of modern Russia.

In time, Kiev overshadowed Rurik's settlement at Novgorod as a trading city. In 879, a Varangian named Oleg, a successor to Rurik, arrived in Kiev from Novgorod and killed both Askold and Dir. For the next 33 years, Oleg ruled a widespread Viking colony that included both Russian trading centers. Known as "the Wise One," he extended his authority and rule over many Slavic tribes. Always a successful and ambitious ruler, he even mounted a military campaign against the crossroads trading city of Constantinople in 907. The *Primary Chronicle* describes the extent of Oleg's assault on the most powerful trading center between Europe and Asia:

> With [his] entire force, Oleg sallied forth by horse and by ship, and the number of his vessels was two thousand. He arrived before Tsar'grad [Constantinople], but the Greeks fortified the strait and closed up the city. Oleg disembarked upon the shore, and ordered his soldiery to beach the ships. . . . The Russes inflicted many . . . woes upon the Greeks after the usual manner of soldiers. Oleg commanded his warriors to make wheels which they attached to the ships, and when the wind was favorable, they spread the sails and bore down upon the city from the open country. When the Greeks beheld this, they were afraid, and sending messengers to Oleg, they implored him not to destroy the city and offered to submit such tribute as he should desire.[20]

The tribute Oleg exacted was high, an amount equivalent to 12 silver coins for each of the 40 men on his 2,000 ships.

Oleg did not remain in Constantinople after this. Having gained much in tribute, both immediate and promised for the future, he returned to Kiev, "bearing palls, gold, fruit, and wine, along with every sort of adornment."[21]

It should be noted that, through these years of political rivalry among the Vikings in Russia, an important trend was established. Rurik had settled in power early in Novgorod—which was located along the banks of Lake Ilmen—and had placed some of his relations in power over other important Viking communities in the region, including Pskov and Rostov. In the meantime, Askold and Dir smartly placed themselves in control of another Russian trade center, Kiev, which "was strategically located on the border of the forest and steppe zone in the center of the waterways, flowing north and south, and which was within easy reach of the great civilized metropolis Constantinople."[22]

When Oleg succeeded Rurik, he, too, recognized the significance of Kievan power and occupied Kiev for himself. By taking control of Kiev, Oleg combined his previous landholdings in the north with the southern center, with Kiev as the base. Thus, historians credit Oleg with having established a true "Russia." Today, he is considered the founder and father of the Russian state. Historian Walther Kirchner sums up the impact of Oleg's shift of power to Kiev:

> Oleg's transfer of central authority to Kiev shifted the balance from Novgorod, with its dependence upon the Baltic Sea, to the south, with its Black Sea connections. Although the steppe country on the Black Sea could not be retained or recovered from invading Asiatic tribes, the mouth of the Dnieper was secured and the whole course of the river brought into "Russian" hands. From Kiev, trade routes were kept open, not only with Constantinople but also with the Volga region. At this period, the future of Russia for the next three centuries becomes evident.[23]

By 912, Oleg was dead. He was followed as ruler by Igor, who was either the son or grandson of Rurik. This grand prince of Kiev was ruthless but effective. He managed to subdue rebellions within and invasions against his state alike. He ordered another attack against Constantinople in 944, but Islamic diplomats negotiated with him and other Viking leaders and managed to stave off the assault. The following year, Igor was killed in another campaign by his longtime enemies, the Derevlians, an East Slavic tribe. He was succeeded by his son, Svyatoslav I, who carried out extraordinary war campaigns against the Khazars along the Don River and the Bulgars along the Volga and Danube Rivers. Svyatoslav attempted to extend the territory of the Kievan Rus throughout the Volga region.

By 967, Svyatoslav's Viking followers had conquered northern Bulgaria. He became legendary for his mobility and personal austerity while on a march: "Upon his expeditions he carried with him neither wagons nor kettles, and boiled no meat, but cut off small strips of horseflesh, game, or beef, and ate it after roasting it on the coals. Nor did he have a tent, but he spread out a horse-blanket under him, and set his saddle under his head."[24] His years of military leadership were cut short when, in the early 970s, he died while fighting the Pechenegs, "whose chief had [Svyatoslav's] skull made into a gold-encrusted drinking cup."[25] Svyatoslav had not reached the tenth year of his rule. After his death, the lands of the Rus were divided among his three sons: Oleg, who ruled the Derevlians; Vladimir, ruler of Novgorod; and Yaropolk, whose reign was centered in Kiev.

This three-way rule of the vast Viking holdings in Russia did not remain intact for long. Prince Vladimir became a ruthless autocrat who ultimately wrested power from his siblings, whom he killed. As the new voice of the Kievan Rus, Vladimir pursued ambitious expansionism, including the capture of

Polish communities in western Ukraine and the defeat of Lithuanian tribesmen along the Neman River.

THE MAKING OF VIKING LEGEND

Written records that refer to the Vikings in Russia are rare today. One fascinating surviving text was penned by an Arab diplomat named Ibn Fadlan. During the 920s, the Arab ruler of Baghdad sent Fadlan on a mission, called a *risala*, to the eastern lands of the Swedish Vikings. He was to make contact with the tribal leader of the Bulgars who lived along a stretch of land that flanked the banks of the Middle Volga River. While there, Fadlan came in contact with a tribe of Norse merchants and shippers who had settled in the area of modern-day Russia, people the visiting Arab diplomat called "the Rus." His descriptions of these strange people from the northlands of Europe are most revealing:

> I have seen the Rus as they came in on their merchant journeys and encamped on the Volga. I have never seen more perfect physical specimens, tall as date palms, blond and ruddy; they wear neither tunics nor caftans, but the men wear a garment that covers one side of the body and leaves a hand free. Each man has an ax, a sword, and a knife, and keeps each by him at all times. . . . Each woman wears on either breast a box of iron, silver, copper or gold . . . each box has a ring from which hangs a knife. The women wear neck-rings of gold and silver . . . their most prized ornaments are green glass beads.[26]

During his visit with these Volga traders, Fadlan witnessed a funeral for a wealthy Rus leader. His account describes a ship cremation, a practice that centered on the "burial at sea" of a noted Norseman by placing his corpse onboard his ship and then setting the vessel on fire. With rich detail, Fadlan presented the strange scene before him:

> I had heard that at the deaths of their chief personages they did many things, of which the least was cremation, and I was interested to learn more. . . . When a great personage dies, his family asks his young women and men slaves, "Who among you will die with him?" One answered, "I".
>
> . . . Now they took her to the ship. She took off the two bracelets she was wearing and gave them both to the old woman called the Angel of Death who was to kill her. . . . They laid her at her master's side. Two held her feet and two her hands. The old woman . . . looped a cord round her neck, and gave the crossed ends to two of the men to pull. Then she came forward with a broad-bladed dagger and plunged it over and over again between her ribs, while the two men strangled her with the cord until she was dead.
>
> Then the closest relative of the dead man came and took a piece of lighted wood. . . . He walked backwards to the ship, holding the torch in his hand, and set fire to the pile of wood beneath the ship. . . . Thereupon the flames engulfed the wood, then the ship . . . the man, the girl and everything in the ship.[27]

THE VOLGA SILVER ROUTE

One direct benefit the Swedish Vikings gained through their voyages into the Russian interior was the connection with a variety of lucrative trading routes. Viking traders sailed along nearly every river in the region of the Volga. Some sailed directly east to the lands of the Bulgar tribes and then farther to the Khazar nomads, until they reached the very streets of one of the great Middle Eastern trading capitals of their day: Baghdad. In making contact with the Bulgars, who lived in the great bend along the banks of the Volga, near the present-day city of Kazan, the Norsemen had reached the western terminus of one of the great trading routes to the Orient, the Silk Road. This Asian trade corridor ran to the east until it reached China, and the markets created by connecting Europe with the Far East were enormous and highly profitable. There can be no doubt that Scandinavian merchants and traders far from home made contact with trade caravans along the commercial highway because "Chinese silks have been found in graves at Birka in central Sweden."[28] Other evidence suggests that Rus traders may have made the trip to China themselves and traded directly with Eastern merchants.

One of the great trading commodities that lured the Vikings into the region of the Volga was silver. A great market trading in silver existed at Bulgar; there, Scandinavian merchants saw massive quantities of Arab-produced silver. The silver trade along the Volga at Bulgar may have sprung up as early as the end of the 700s, when trading agreements between Arab tribesmen, known as the Abbasids, and the Khazar tribes of the Lower Volga were made. The Abbasids had taken power in the Islamic world by 750 and established their capital at Baghdad rather than at Damascus, the longstanding center of Arab power. By the time the Vikings were making their way to the region of the Volga, the city of Baghdad had become an extremely wealthy and powerful merchant center and the crossroads for many trading routes. The region surrounding Baghdad and to the east was rich with silver mines. In Afghanistan, huge silver strikes were unearthed by the 800s. Additional mines were producing silver in central Asian states such as Uzbekistan and Tajikistan.

It appears that the Viking Rus began to seriously tap the Arab silver markets by the mid-800s. Scandinavian traders and merchants began to accumulate vast quantities of minted silver coins, some several decades old by the time they slipped into the hands of the Vikings. Through the work of modern-day archaeologists, "over 60,000 Arab coins have been found in over 1,000 hoards in Scandinavia alone, with many others in the Viking colonies."[29] In exchange for the precious metal, the Norsemen traded goods common to their culture, including "furs, slaves, falcons, honey, wax, walrus ivory and strong steel swords."[30] These caches of Arab coins found at Norse sites represent only a small portion of the Vikings' holdings. The majority of the silver coinage acquired by the Vikings was melted down and recast into items such as jewelry and larger silver bars.

The Vikings also traded with the Khazar nomads who lived along the Caspian Sea and controlled the entire region through which the Lower Volga flowed. Silver was always at the center of the Khazar-Viking trade. This trade became extensive as proven by Scandinavian archaeology sites, where items belonging to the Khazars have been uncovered, including types of rings that became commonplace among the Vikings.

By the end of the ninth century, the silver trade between the Vikings and various eastern traders, including the Abbasids and Khazars, was beginning to dwindle. Many of the region's silver mines were exhausted, tapped of their riches by constant and extensive trading among foreigners converging from near and far. By 892, however, some massive silver strikes had been made in Afghanistan, and the trade was revived. A wave of silver found its way into the region's trade and "huge quantities of coins . . . found their way west into Russia and the Viking world."[31] The new silver rush continued throughout the Euroasian region, including the vicinity of the Volga, for another century. Archaeologists have excavated even more Russian sites with greater quantities of Arab silver coins than in earlier sites. By the 980s and 990s, this second silver boom was over, and the Vikings, who had settled and colonized throughout the Volga River system and beyond for several centuries, looked elsewhere for new riches.

By 1015, many of the old trade connections between the Rus and the Arabs had been completely abandoned. "Silver" coins continued to circulate across late-tenth-century Kievan Russia during the final decades of Viking influence, but the coins were becoming debased as their silver content was drastically reduced during the eleventh century. Even as late as A.D. 1000, the silver content of the trade coins was 90 percent. A century later, the silver content had been reduced to about 5 percent.

THE DECLINE OF KIEVAN RUSSIA

The ruthless Viking ruler-prince Vladimir died in 1015 and was followed by Sviatopluk "the Accursed," who ruled as grand prince of Kiev. Viking power in the region gradually waned over the next two centuries. This period was high-lighted by constant problems among the ruling families of Kiev and the Viking-controlled region of the Volga. There was much infighting, which sometimes pitted royal brother against royal brother. During the century after Vladimir's death, only two Kievan rulers stand above the others as reasonable men who led successfully: Yaroslav the Wise and Vladimir II Monomachus.

Yaroslav the Wise ruled from 1019 to 1054. Noted as a man of letters and a scholar, he established libraries and schools, encouraged and supported translations of ancient Greek texts and manuscripts, and was a patron of the arts. During his reign, he ordered the construction of significant Kievan monuments such as the Churches of St. George, St. Catherine, and St. Sophia, the grandest of them all. He became noted for his support of the codification of old Russian laws. After Yaroslav's death, Kievan Russia experienced decades of "brutal, gruesome feuds and disrupting civil wars."[32] Vladimir II Monomachus rose to the throne 60 years after Yaroslav's rule and managed to reunite his fractured state using Yaroslav's rule as the model for his own. He worked hard to keep the peace in his state while extending Kievan trade connections. (For additional information on this enlightened Russian ruler, enter "Yaroslav the Wise" into any search engine and browse the many sites listed.)

Old patterns of royal mismanagement surfaced after the rule of Vladimir II's son, Mstislav I. Rivalries among various princes became commonplace, resulting in disunion. While princes vied for power, it fell to the towns scattered throughout Kievan Russia to preserve law and order. The general assemblies that held control of the more important communities were dominated by freemen called *vieche*, and these individuals became the backbone of progressive politics in Russia from the 1100s through the fourteenth century. Towns such as Novgorod, Polotsk, Pskov, Rostov, Smolensk, and Suzdal became increasingly important trade communities; some even rivaling Kiev. As such towns gained power and independence, the princes ruling from Kiev began to feel the impact of their collective weight. In time, the princes had to be responsive to the will of these communities to retain true power. Kiev "was gradually reduced to the position of but one of many important places, and after three hundred years of predominance even this position was lost in the thirteenth century."[33]

As Russian princes witnessed the decline of Kiev, they realized that they had to establish a new power base, one removed from the southern Russian region and the Dnieper basin. In search of a new capital, they immigrated to the northeast, into the region of the Upper Volga and its primary tributaries. Suzdal was selected as the first capital, and the grand princes abandoned Kiev. Suzdal was followed by the town of Vladimir, near the Volga River, where strong-handed Prince Andrew Bogolyubsky, grand duke of Suzdal, established the capital in 1157.

Yaroslav the Wise, who ruled Kiev from 1019 to 1054, erected the cathedrals of St. George, St. Catherine, and St. Sophia, which is located in Novgorod and shown here. Completed in 1045, St. Sophia was the first church in Russia that included the distinctive onion-shaped domes—which signify a flame of a candle burning upward toward heaven—synonymous with the Russian Orthodox Church.

Neither capital site proved viable. Each was, in its own way, "less favorably located than Kiev had been."[34] Despite royal attempts to stave off the further decline of Kievan Russia, the kingdom continued to collapse. Over the next two centuries, nearly all of western Russia slipped out of the hands of the grand dukes. By 1400, the state of "Kievan Russia" comprised little more than the territory surrounding Suzdal. These lands were called "Muscovy" because the Russian royalty had by then moved its capital to another site: Moscow.

The Golden Horde

With the collapse of Kiev, the Russian state was seriously weakened and became increasingly vulnerable to attack by foreign invaders. These invaders soon swarmed into the region of the Volga specifically and across Russia in general. They came from the east, from Asian Mongolia, a mysterious land to many Russians, and when these horsemen turned their eyes to the west and began to invade, they "came upon the Russians like a bolt from the blue." [35] Many historical sources have referred to these furious and highly mobile warrior invaders as the Tatars. More modern scholars and historians know them as the Mongols.

The Mongols first arrived in 1223, when they rode into southeastern Russia and met the Russians in a battle that raged along the banks of the Kalka River; but these Mongol cavalrymen returned to the west and vanished into the Asian steppes. The real invasion came in the late 1230s, and it was marked by extreme brutality. One contemporary writer recorded the raid on the river city of Riazan, on the Oka, a tributary of the Volga. He drew a vivid, terrifying account of the slaughter exacted by the Mongols:

> The churches of God they devastated, and in the holy altars they shed much blood. And no one in the town remained alive: all died equally and drank the single cup of death. There was no one here to moan or cry—neither father and mother over children, nor children over father and mother, neither brother over brother, nor relatives over relatives— but all lay together dead. [36]

Such devastation was repeated again and again as the Mongols spent years subjugating the Russian peoples. Who, then, were these Asian invaders who called themselves "the Golden Horde"?

THE MONGOLIAN KHANS

For hundreds of years, Mongolian-speaking tribes had lived in present-day Mongolia, Manchuria, and Siberia and were unknown to the Russians who lived far to the west. At the beginning of the thirteenth century, several scattered tribes living in the Mongolian desert, including Mongol and Turkic peoples, banded together to form a single formidable fighting unit. Their prowess for war soon instilled fear in their neighbors to the south, the Chinese. One Chinese writer penned his impressions of the newly formed Mongolian war machine:

> From childhood they practice riding and shooting arrows . . . and thus they acquire courage necessary for pillage and war. As long as they hope for success, they move back and forth; . . . Religious rites and legal institutions they know not. . . . They all feed on the meat of the animals which they kill . . . and they dress in their hides and furs. The strongest among them grab the fattest pieces; the old men, on the other hand, eat and drink what is left. They respect only the bravest; old age and feebleness are held in contempt.[37]

Early in the thirteenth century, a man who would lead the Golden Horde in an expansive conquest across Asia emerged. His birth name was Temujin, and he began his military-political career as a minor chieftain. Through a series of intertribal wars, Temujin was able to unite "first his clan, then his tribe, and finally the majority of tribes . . . in his support."[38] In 1206, once he had gained position and power, an assembly of chieftains declared Temujin the "genghis khan," which translates as "all-encompassing lord."

The coalition of tribesmen that Temujin, now known as Genghis Khan, formed under his leadership was one of extraordinary skill and fortitude. Mongol boys were placed in the saddle at age three, when their early instruction in the use of

In 1223, Genghis Khan and the Mongols reached the Lower Volga region, where they defeated a group of Cumans (a Turkish people) and Russians on the Kalka River. Fortunately for the Russians, the Mongols returned to Mongolia, where Genghis died four years later. This memorial to the great Mongol leader is in Elista, Russia, near the Caspian Sea.

the bow and arrow commenced. At the center of the developing reputation of the Mongol horsemen were the horses themselves. They were strong Mongol ponies that required no special feeding but could sustain themselves by foraging for food, even scrub grasses buried under winter and high mountain snows. The Mongols understood the importance of their mounts and took great care of them. Each Mongol warrior owned a small herd of horses, and when he went on a raid or other campaign, a Mongol fighter might have as many as 20 fresh horses he could mount, making himself and his comrades extremely mobile. This was the most important tactic used by the followers of Genghis Khan.

Once Genghis Khan had united the Mongols, he launched an invasion of China in 1211 and managed to punch through the Great Wall, which had been erected as a defensive measure. Over the next five years, Genghis Khan, with perhaps as many as 100,000 horsebound warriors at his disposal, conquered 100 million Chinese. He then began an invasion of the Muslim states of central Asia, smashing them easily, and advanced south to the Caspian Sea and then north into the Caucasus. By 1223, the Mongols had slipped through the mountain passes of the region and reached the Russian people known as the Cumans, a Turkish group living in the vicinity of the Lower Volga. Frightened of the Mongols, the Cuman khans appealed to neighboring Russian princes to assist them in resisting the horsemen of the Golden Horde. In their messages, they wrote, "Today the Tatars [Mongols] have seized our land. Tomorrow they will take yours."[39] Several Russian princes, including Prince Mstislav of Galicia, responded and sent men to fight the Mongols.

On the northeastern end of the Sea of Azov, along the banks of the Kalka River, the Cumans and Russians engaged the Mongols in battle. The fight was a lopsided Mongol victory. Most were killed by the forces of Genghis Khan, and Mstislav and several other Russian princes were captured. They were not spared, but, as royalty, their deaths were to be bloodless, a rule applied to the executions of Mongol chieftains. In accordance with Mongol law and tradition, the Russian princes were laid on the ground and boards were placed on top of them, forming a platform "upon which the Mongol officers sat for their victory banquet," [40] crushing the Russian royalty.

Genghis Khan and his men did not remain in the Volga region but returned to their homelands. As one relieved Russian writer chronicled: "We do not know whence these evil Tatars came upon us, nor whither they have betaken themselves again; only God knows." [41] Genghis Khan never returned to Russia; he died four years later while on a campaign against the Tibetans. Before his death, he had ordered that his leadership be passed into the hands of his sons Juji, the eldest, and his younger brother, Ogadai. Juji had died before his father, however, so his portion of the land fell to his son, Batu. The lands Juji had been granted included the region west of the Aral Sea, most of which had not actually been conquered by the Mongols. With his uncle's approval, Batu picked up where his father and grandfather had left off. In 1236, he took a Mongolian cavalry force to the west. His invasion would change Russian history forever.

Under Batu's leadership, the Mongolians raided beyond the Caspian Sea and turned north. They captured Bulgary, the capital of the Volga Bulgars, and although the Russian winter soon set in, Batu's force of 50,000 horsemen continued to advance. Accustomed to living under difficult conditions, the Mongols emerged from the forests and used frozen riverbeds as roads. They next laid siege to the town of Riazan. Unable to defend themselves against a winter assault, the people of Riazan surrendered in less than a week, on December 21, 1237. The slaughter was intense. Some of the Russian victims "were impaled or had nails or splinters of wood driven under their finger nails. Priests were roasted alive and nuns and maidens were ravished in the churches before their relatives."[42] The Mongolians believed that, by taking such actions, they were completing the mission of Genghis Khan, the "Great Khan," whom God had ordered to conquer the world and its inhabitants. Anyone who stood in their way was defying the will of God and had to be punished.

Within two months, the Mongols raided and brought down 14 Russian towns and villages, including several on the Volga, such as Tver. Then they advanced on to the Russian trade city of Novgorod. Only when Batu and his men found the forests and swamps blocking their way did they forego conquering Novgorod, deciding instead to return to the Russian steppes to the east. Batu continued to bring down other towns. One community, Kozelsk, held out for nearly two months. When the city finally fell, the Mongols were so incensed by the delay that they slaughtered every being—human and animal alike— in the city. According to one written account, "blood was so deep in the streets . . . that children drowned before they could be slain."[43]

The year 1238 saw a dramatic succession of military victories for Batu and his armies. He let his men rest the following year, but by 1240, he was ready to continue his western campaign across a terrified Russia. The cities of Pereyaslavl and Chernigov were destroyed, and Batu soon set his eye on the important Russian political and trade center of Kiev. When the Mongolian leader dispatched representatives from his camp to deliver an ultimatum to the Russian governor, the local ruler ordered the envoys to be executed. This reckless move sealed the fate of Kiev. Batu laid siege yet again—this time in December 1240— and the struggle lasted only a few days. One of the grandest cities in all of Europe fell under the sword of the invading Mongols. The devastation was complete, and thousands were slaughtered. Six years after Batu's destruction of Kiev, a traveler to the region,

Archbishop Giovanni da Plano Carpini, wrote an account of the aftermath of Batu's attack:

> [T]hey went against Russia and enacted a great massacre in the Russian land, they destroyed towns and fortresses and killed people, they besieged Kiev which had been the capital of Russia, and after a long siege they took it and killed the inhabitants of the city; for this reason, when we passed through that land, we found lying in the field countless heads and bones of dead people; for this city had been extremely large and very populous, whereas now it has been reduced to nothing: barely two hundred houses stand there, and those people are held in the harshest slavery.[44]

Undaunted by his distance from Mongolia, Batu ordered his men farther west and even divided his forces, sending them scattering in several directions. One unit pushed into Poland; another rode hard toward the Carpathian Mountains into southern Hungary. Batu personally led a third into northern Hungary. His two split-off armies provided long-range protection for both of his flanks. Soon, all of Hungary was swarmed by Mongol horsemen, as were the lands of Poland, Lithuania, and East Prussia. Even the city of Vienna was captured.

In 1242, as Batu eyed new targets in western Europe, he received word of the death of his uncle, the Great Khan Ogadai. The great Mongolian leader stopped the advance of his forces and announced his intent to return to his homeland. A new khan was to be chosen, and Batu intended to take up the vacant leadership position. He returned to the east through Bulgaria, completing a great, sweeping circle around eastern and central Europe.

Years of campaigning, slaughtering, and conquering all resistance by the Russians and others had led him back to the Volga steppes. Batu had not only conquered the southern

Russian steppes and the forestlands of northern Russia, he also had reached the sparkling blue waters of the Danube River. Although Hungary had been overrun, it remained a Mongolian province for less than a year. Other lands he had defeated—including Bulgaria and Moldavia—remained in Mongolian hands for more than a century. During these same years, other Mongolian armies had managed to defeat the northern provincial Chinese and the people living in the Transcaucasus. A vast, imperial Mongolian province, called a *ulus*, had been built on strong leadership and a great amount of blood. It stretched from the Adriatic Sea east to the distant Pacific Ocean.

Despite Batu's successes across the lands of Eurasia, he did not inherit his uncle's throne. Although Ogadai had selected Batu as his successor before his death, the khan's wife conspired to bring her own son, Kuyuk, to the Mongolian throne. Out of loyalty, Batu did not challenge his cousin's right to the position of the khanship. Although he remained loyal to the Great Khan Kuyuk, he never returned to Mongolia to pay his respects. He remained along the banks of the Volga River, ruling over his conquered lands, which remained a province of the Mongol-Tatar Empire. He and those who followed him as successors practiced a significant level of independence from the khanate of Kuyuk.

Even before the death of Ogadai and the rise of Kuyuk, Batu had established himself a capital at the Russian site of Sarai, 65 miles north of Astrakhan, along the Lower Volga. Sarai was a strategic location: Situated near where the steppes and the surrounding desert lands join, it flanked the Volga in a region where the great Russian river and its neighbor, the Don, flowed close to one another. It was also close to the Black Sea. In its early stages, the settlement at Sarai was nothing more than a tent city, because Batu was never certain when he and his men might need to pack up their community and take up arms in yet another campaign of conquest or, perhaps, reconquest. Despite the seeming impermanence of the city, the court of

Batu was legendary for its lavishness. A contemporary writer described its pomp and grandeur:

> Batu lives with considerable magnificence, having door-keepers and all officials just like their Emperor. He even sits raised up as if on a throne with one of his wives. . . . He has large and very beautiful tents of linen which used to belong to the King of Hungary. . . . Drinks are placed in gold and silver vessels. Neither Batu nor any other Tatar prince ever drinks, especially in public, without there being singing and guitar-playing for them.[45]

CENTURIES OF MONGOLIAN RULE

From his capital at Sarai, Batu ruled over a nearly autonomous Mongolian state, the Golden Horde. His lands stretched across the landscape of Russia and elsewhere, including the homeland of the Volga-Kama Bulgars; the lands of the Cumans, situated along the Black Sea steppes; the northern Caucasus; and the Asian lands of western Siberia and Khorezm (modern-day Turkistan).

To maintain his court and his control over the people of his province, Batu established an extensive taxation system. At first, he dispatched his own tax collectors across the Golden Horde, and they met with general success. Any community that did not pay the taxes knew that they would face his wrath and destruction at the hands of his armies. Because Batu levied taxes directly, he had to order several censuses to get an exact headcount. The Mongols took a census three times during the thirteenth century, the last one in 1275. Batu and his successors also used censuses as a means of conscripting men into the Mongolian military. These Russian troops were deployed everywhere within Mongolians provinces, including as far away as southern China.

THE ORIGINS OF THE GOLDEN HORDE

The Mongolian province established by Batu and his conquering horsemen from 1237 through 1241 was extensive, stretching from Russia to neighboring European states to the west. As he established his kingdom, the term "Golden Horde" began to be used as a label for the province.

The term is an intriguing one. To what did the phrase—and all its romantic implications—refer? What was "golden" about the province established by Batu? To be certain, the province was destined to become quite wealthy. Batu's agents collected taxes and Russian princes lavished wealth on his state as forced tribute—but the gold paid in taxes is not the "golden" portion of the province's name.

The name is more indicative of royalty than of monetary wealth. As one historian explains, "The Mongol stronghold on the steppe was known as the Golden Horde, not because it was the base of a swarm of yellow-skinned warriors, but because yellow was the imperial color of the khan and his clan."[*]

Some scholars have suggested that the significance of the golden color was derived from the symbolism the Chinese place on specific colors. The ancient Chinese identified the cardinal points of the compass with certain colors. Black was symbolic of north, red was the color of the south, the east was blue, and white was the color to indicate the west. Yellow was known as an imperial color, the symbolic shade that represented the center of all things. The explanation of the word "horde" is more straightforward. In Mongolian, the word "horde" comes from the word *ordu*, which translates as "encampment."

The name Golden Horde was used as an identification for the state established by Batu, but another name, one that recognized the importance of Batu's father, Juji, was also used. The lands were known as Juji's Ulus. With the passage of time and the dimming of the memory of Juji among the Mongolians who controlled the Russian-centered province, the name Golden Horde became singular and commonplace, a term that lives on through the pages of history.

[*] Grey, *Horizon History*, 48.

The Mongols originally relied on their own tax collectors to obtain money from the Russians under their yoke, but they soon altered their policy and allowed local Russian princes to collect taxes for them. Each prince who was granted the privilege first had to pay a visit to Sarai. (Sometimes they were obliged to make a great journey to Karakoram in Mongolia, the capital of Kuyuk and other later great khans.) The Russian leaders then received a *yarkyk*, or official charter. It translates from Russian as a "customs stamp," taken from a Mongolian word referring to the written decrees of the khan, especially a decree that bestowed a privilege. The yarkyk recognized members of the Russian royalty as the true leaders of each of their royal realms, with the understanding that each Russian prince was also serving at the permission of the Mongol khans. The value of a yarkyk, beyond the stamp of approval for a local prince's power, was that sanctioned Russian leaders could order their people to pay taxes higher than that expected by the Mongolians, leaving the surplus in the hands of the princes. Seeking this privilege, Russian princes vigorously competed with one another, often resorting to "extremes of self-humiliation, bribery, treachery and violence. In their continuing feuds the princes also sought, and frequently got, the military aid of the Mongols against their own kinsmen." [46]

Allowing favored Russian princes the power to collect taxes was profitable for the Mongolians because the policy helped them cut down on bureaucratic expenses and keep their political structures to a minimum. This allowed them to utilize the Russian lands at their disposal in the ways they wanted—largely as a source of taxation and military manpower. By leaving the Russian hierarchical system of royalty, aristocracy, and farming peasantry intact, however, the Mongolians made the mistake of leaving the very groups that would one day overthrow Mongolian rule in place; often patiently biding their time, wait-ing for the right moment to challenge the authority and power of their conquerors. The wait was a long one. Many decades, even centuries, passed before the complete removal of Mongolian power across Russia and in the Volga River region.

The Mongolians did not interfere much with the daily lives of the Russian people, but they did rule over them for approximately 250 years. The occupation held back Russian progress, as the Mongolians "deprived the Russians for centuries of much of the best land and contributed to the shift of population, economic activity, and political power to the northeast." [47] Occasionally, the Russians attempted rebellions and protests against Mongol taxes, but these were typically put down harshly. As early as the middle of the 1300s, however, protests and challenges aimed at the Mongolian rulers began to disturb the iron-fisted control of the Asian overlords.

By the 1370s, the grand duke of Moscow, Dimitri, rallied the Russian people against the ruling khan, Mamai, and refused to pay the annual tribute. When Mongolian leaders responded by sending an army backed by Lithuanian allies to teach the Muscovites a lesson, other Russian princes gave support and military aid, sending no fewer than 150,000 fighters. The Russian church sanctioned the rebellion, and others were encouraged to join in the fight. When Dimitri finally moved in the field, ready to loose the Mongolian stranglehold on his people, he met 200,000 Mongol-led troops along the confluence of the Don and the Nepryadva Rivers. In the battle of Kulikovo, the Mongols were defeated but at a heavy cost to Dimitri's army. When the battle was over, only 40,000 "able-bodied survivors were left, and Dimitri himself was found half dead among a pile of corpses, his armor shattered and pounded in." [48]

Dimitri did survive, but the victory at Kulikovo was not decisive, and the Mongolians continued to rule. Two years later, a Mongolian army attacked Moscow in Dimitri's absence and killed tens of thousands. When the Russian rebel prince

In the late fourteenth century, Dimitri Ivanovich, the grand duke of Moscow, helped expand Muscovy territory thanks to an ever-weakening Mongol presence in Russia. Seen here is a mural that depicts the blessing of Dimitri before he leaves for the battle of Kulikovo in 1380. Dimitri's forces defeated a Mongol army led by Mamai, but the Mongols continued to rule Russia for another hundred years.

reached the devastated city, he paid for the burial of nearly 25,000 Russians, yet further fighting between Dimitri's forces and the Mongolians did not materialize. After ruling a rebellious Russia for a century and a half, the Mongolians were tired—and disunited. In fact, the next significant fighting that occurred on Russian soil was an attack against the Golden Horde by another Mongolian, Timur the Lame, known as Tamerlane, who was extending his own Mongolian kingdom across Asia, challenging the entrenched, old-line Mongolian leaders in Sarai. After his defeat of his fellow Mongolians during the 1390s, Tamerlane did not remain in Russia long. After advancing to within 200 miles of Moscow, he was turned away by reports that the Russians were entrenched in large numbers in his path. He ordered a retreat and slipped out of Russia, leaving a crushed Golden Horde behind. (For additional information on this Mongol Khan, enter "Khan Tamerlane" into any search engine and browse the many sites listed.)

Mongolian rule over the Russians in the Volga and Don region never fully recovered. By the early 1400s, the rule of the Golden Horde began to decline steadily. Dimitri's son and successor, Vasily I, refused to pay tribute to Sarai. Throughout his lengthy reign (1389 to 1425), Vasily expanded his own royal power by campaigning to the west—fighting constantly against the Lithuanians, who had become allied with the Mongols. He also fought against the principality of Tver, on the Volga, and forced its leaders to recognize his power and authority as the leader of Moscow. Slowly, the power of the Mongols was broken, unraveling to its ultimate demise.

Some of the destruction of the Golden Horde was caused by factions among the Mongols themselves. In 1445, the Tatar kingdom of Kazan declared its autonomy from the Golden Horde. Within a few years, the Crimean Tatars did the same, further weakening the power of the old Mongolian kingdom. The ultimate death knell for the Golden Horde was delivered by a Russian, a princely grandson of Vasily I and founder of tsarist power—Ivan III of Moscow.

5

The Rise of the Tsars

Af...fter experiencing more than 250 years of oppression at the hands of the Tatars (the Mongols), the Russians and their princely leaders had reached their breaking point. In 1437, the Tatar ruler, Ula Mehmet, was removed from the leadership of the Golden Horde on the Lower Volga and fled north to establish another Mongolian state, called Kazan. The garrison he ordered his followers to build was formidable— the greatest fortress the Mongols held between Moscow and the Urals. Perhaps as many as 30,000 soldiers were posted at Mehmet's fortress. For a generation or so, Russian princes paid tribute to the Mongol leader, biding their time until they could challenge his power. The formal end of Tatar sovereignty over Russia came in 1480 with a battle that unfolded along the banks of the Oka River; one that brought defeat to the Asian overlords. The collapse of the Mongolian Empire in Russia coincided with the rise of an aristocratic Russian leader, Ivan III (also known as Ivan the Great), who reigned from 1462 to 1505.

During 40 years of rule, Ivan, with the support of his wife, Sophia, managed to create a new style of leadership. Sophia was a niece of the last Byzantine emperor, Constantine XI. In 1453, the city of Constantinople fell at the hands of the Seljuk Turks. With the fall of the 1,000-year-old empire of Byzantium, Sophia encouraged Ivan to claim the fallen emperorship. In time, Ivan claimed the title of "tsar" (a derivation of the old Roman title "imperator," which is often referred to in history as "caesar"). The Russian leader adopted the symbol of the black two-headed eagle, formerly the symbol of the Byzantine Empire (and the Persian Empire in an earlier time), and turned it into the symbol of the Muscovite state. Also, Ivan claimed power over the Russian church, which became independent of the Patriarchate of Constantinople shortly before the fall of the Byzantine Empire. Before his death, Ivan III had transformed himself into the supreme ruler of Russia, and his capital of Moscow, situated in the region of the Upper Volga on the Oka River, was the new seat of power. Through shrewd political jockeying, Ivan was able to extend the borders of his kingdom to include thousands of additional square miles of territory to the north and the northeast, even beyond the banks of the Volga to the east. Before his reign was over, he had added more than 50,000 square miles of territory to the domain of Moscovy.

Ivan III's reign was followed by that of his son, Basil III, which lasted from 1505 to 1533. Basil picked up where his father had left off, taking more lands for his kingdom, regaining Smolensk from the Poles, and annexing Riazan. Eventually, the Tatar khans in Russia were subdued, became local rulers, and accepted the ascendancy of true Russian leaders. The khans of Krim and Nogai and the Volga peoples came to cooperate with the rulers of Moscow. The Volga Tatars became satisfied to rule over rich trade towns along the river, such as Kazan and Astrakhan.

During the late fifteenth and early sixteenth centuries, the Volga River came under the control of the grand dukes such as Ivan III, who ruled from Moscow, which had become the primary city of the region. Various Russian leaders launched military campaigns to secure the great Russian waterway for their trade and national security. Historian Harold Lamb summed up the importance this new generation of Russian leaders placed on the Volga:

> In the century before, Muscovite territory had grown haphazard outward from the Moskva—down the Klaizma along the Oka to the Volga. And in the same way, it had stretched northerly along the upper Volga, taking in at first the plain of the two rivers. It happened that by controlling the territory around cities like Vladimir, Moscow had brought Vladimir into its fold, with the rest of them. Now,

in turn, by holding a city like . . . Novgorod, where the Oka flowed into the Volga, the *trade* of the upper Volga became subject to Moscow control.[49]

Russians began migrating from the forestlands of the extreme north toward the Kama River, where Tatars had only recently ruled, and established themselves along the Volga. Many of these new arrivals were farmers, hunters, and homesteaders who sought the rich, fertile agricultural lands of the region. Soldiers under orders from Ivan III protected these land seekers. This great regional and commercial trend continued under Basil.

The transformation that Russian control of the entire Volga region had on the economy could be seen by the early 1500s. Sigismund von Herberstein, an Austrian ambassador to Moscow, first arrived in the Muscovite capital in 1516, reaching the gates of the city in the company of 15 nobles and 30 servants. During the year that followed, he kept extraordinarily detailed notes about the Russian people, life in Moscow, and the lively trade throughout the region of the Volga and its tributaries. Of this, he wrote: "This convenience of navigation upon the rivers is the cause of the great wealth of the merchants of the country, who are able to transport goods by them, as from the Caspian up the Volga into different regions, and even up as far as Moscow."[50]

Indeed, the Volga was the center of Russian trade. This extraordinary exchange of goods was not limited to the Russian people themselves but was an international trade based on the land and its bounty. In examining the lands around the Oka and the Volga, Herberstein noted that they constituted a "spot so fertile that from one bushel of wheat twenty, or even thirty may be produced."[51] Tatar merchants arrived along the Volga from the east and north, and they met in the river towns to do business with not only Russians but also Swedes and Livonians.

Often, the most important trading centers on the Volga were the local fairs conducted from one small town to the next. The visiting Austrian diplomat noted that towns along the Volga River and its tributaries held more fairs than villages situated away from the rivers. The trade was typically done on the barter system, where "scarcely any use [is] made of gold or silver [coin]."[52] Furs were the prime trade item, for which people would barter homespun clothing, knives and spoons, tools, and other items.

Everyone, including the poor, brought trade items to the river to sell. The banks of the Volga and its feeder rivers were places where "boats would be lined up in such a mass that you could walk from bank to bank over the shipping —on log rafts and luggers."[53] Trading along the rivers featured more colorful exchange than can be imagined. It was along the river that "Finnish hunters could barter skins for the carpets of bearded Turks from the Volga, river men had sturgeon's roe to offer for Tatar boots, Swedes from beyond Ladoga could trade iron plows for the honey of Russian farmers."[54]

Such trade was taking place along the Volga and across the Russian state of Muscovy under the watchful eyes of rulers such as Ivan III and Basil. Soon, another Russian, a true tsar in every sense of the word, would extend his power further throughout the lands fed by the waters of the Volga. He was the son of Basil and the grandson of Ivan III—Ivan IV.

In addition to pursuing an extensive domestic agenda as tsar, Ivan IV (known as Ivan the Terrible) set out to consolidate and extend Russian geopolitical power even farther than his father and grandfather. Although they had broken the back of the Mongolian presence in Russia, there were smaller khanates who still were in control of certain towns on Russian soil, including Kazan. Ivan IV became determined to capture all such Mongol centers of power and trade.

(continued on page 61)

THE BLOODLESS BATTLE ALONG THE OKA

During his first 18 years as grand duke of Russia, Ivan III (the Great) worked hard to avoid a serious, pitched battle against the last significant Tatar outpost, established at Kazan. He paid bribes and tribute to keep the peace. Through those years, however, Ivan also tried to drive a wedge between the few remaining remnants of the Golden Horde along the Lower Volga and the Tatars to the north. By the late 1470s, the king of Poland and the Tatars living along the Volga joined forces and began planning a campaign against Ivan III's stronghold at Moscow, and by 1480, Ivan could no longer steer clear of an all-out military conflict with the Mongols on his soil. Soon, a large Mongol army was marching across the Don River to the Oka, headed for Moscow.

Ivan's first strategy was to send his agents to the Tatars living along the Crimea to raid the hometowns of the Volga Tatars, many of which were defenseless because a large number of soldiers were on the march to Moscow. The tactic did not go as Ivan had planned. The reluctant grand duke—a man of weak military will—came to realize that he would have to gather a force of his own and meet the Mongols on the field of battle.

After sending his wife and their children away to safety, he left Moscow to take command of his forces camped along the Oka River. After he arrived, he was seized by a fit of cowardice and fled back to Moscow. The local citizenry preparing the local fortress, the Kremlin, for a siege, chastised their leader, accused him of fear in the face of the enemy, and shamed him into returning to his troops.

Just how cowardly was Ivan III? History provides conflicting answers. At times, he could be quite forceful. At other times, there were rumors that the grand duke was so timid that he was even afraid of the dark. In fact, Ivan's fear of the battlefield was probably grounded in a simple truth—he had no confidence in himself as a military leader, even though most of his officers were ready for a fight against the horsemen of the Golden Horde:

> That was the one thing Ivan would not do. He knew himself to be a coward; this turbulent camp, noisy with altercation, was a torment to him. Across the river waited terror. Ivan's imagination peopled the far bank with dark masses of charging horsemen. . . . The Tatars . . . rode down to the water's edge to taunt the Russians . . . [and] fired cannon

that blazed and smoked, without doing much damage. They sent exploring columns across distant fords, only to be turned back by bands of experienced Muscovite frontiersmen. Still, Ivan would not give his word to cross the river.[*]

For endless weeks, Ivan received continuous requests from his military leaders, church priests, and even his own counselors to take his army across the Oka. Each time, Ivan refused. When some of his advisers, frustrated with their timid leader, suggested that he simply surrender, Ivan willingly agreed, sending ambassadors to the Tatar encampment with gifts and requesting terms of peace with the Tatar khan. Word came back that the Mongol leader expected that "Ivan should come in person to kiss the stirrup of the Khan and pay the tribute he had not paid for nine years."[**] This was more than even the fearful Ivan could agree to.

The armies remained on opposite sides of the Oka for weeks. Fall arrived, the temperatures turned cold, and Ivan finally ordered his men to move—but not against the Tatars. Instead, to the surprise of his army, he signaled a retreat to Moscow. The army, always an undisciplined rabble of troops, agreed to the march, anxious to move—even if it was away from the enemy. Everything indicated that the last battle to oust the Tatars from Russia would never take place, at least while Grand Duke Ivan was heading the army.

Ironically, Ivan's retreat "probably saved Moscow from another devastation."[†] As the Moscovites began their disorderly march back to their capital, the Tatars, perhaps misreading the move, abandoned their river encampment and beat a hasty retreat back to the security of the Volga River. In fact, the Tatars had watched Ivan's army collect more troops with each passing week, and the Asians finally decided to abandon their advance against Moscow, believing that Ivan's army was too large to defeat. Several Mongol troops had even abandoned their comrades and joined the Russians. The "battle of Oka" would go down in history as a fight that never really took place—but it would be the last stand for the Tatars. Within a generation, the last remnants of the Golden Horde were gone.

[*] Lamb, *March of Muscovy*, 85–86.
[**] Ibid., 86.
[†] Ibid., 87.

Ivan IV, also know as Ivan the Terrible, was the first Russian ruler to formally accept the title of tsar. He expanded Russia's territory to the east by conquering the khanates of Kazan and Astrakhan in 1552 and 1556, respectively, and gained control of Siberia in the 1580s.

(continued from page 57)

During the summer of 1552, the Russian tsar gathered a military force of 100,000 men and dozens of cannons and dispatched them to Kazan on boats along the Volga River. In attempting to turn his military advance into a Christian mission, he had a special prayer worded "Lord, in Thy name we go forward."[55] He envisioned his advance on Kazan as "a glorious crusade that would earn him renown as the tsar-liberator who had crushed the Moslems and planted the Cross in Asia."[56] Although his assault on Kazan did not unfold perfectly —he lost many of his boats on the river, as well as most of his supplies and thousands of men—he laid siege to this city, located at the confluence of the Kama and Volga Rivers. For many days, his fighters besieged Kazan as Ivan IV rode among his men, encouraging them to remain at their posts. In time, the great symbolic fortress of the last remnant of the Tatars fell, signaling the beginning of years of territorial expansion for Ivan and his Russian state.

As loyal Muscovites rallied behind their conquering tsar, Muscovy grew and the Tatar presence finally waned. The khanate of Astrakhan, the old Tatar stronghold near the mouth of the Volga River, surrendered his stronghold to Ivan IV by 1556. Such victories over old enemies helped establish a clearer concept of Russian dominance and nationhood. The military victories of the tsar allowed for more land to be annexed, and further Russian colonization followed. New farms sprang up on the "fertile, black soil lands, watered by tributaries of the Volga and the Don."[57] The empire of Ivan IV finally included the entire length of the Volga River to the Caspian Sea. The great river was completely Russian.

Modernization along the Volga

Ivan IV's impact on Russian history was extraordinary. Although born the "grand prince of Moscow" at the age of 3, he declared himself to be more than a prince at age 16, taking on the old Byzantine imperial title "tsar." For decades, the harsh, politically driven Russian autocrat fought to consolidate his power and advance the standing of his country as a leading European state. Progress was made during Ivan's reign, but Russia was still considered backward compared to other European powers. The stage was set, though, thanks to Ivan's successes, for Russia to take its seat among the great kingdoms of Europe. The process of modernizing the Russian state would take hundreds of years; still, change took place, usually at the hands of tsars as forceful as Ivan IV.

When Ivan, known across Russia as a harsh, cruel tyrant, died in 1584, he was followed by a son who was unfit to rule. Three years earlier, in one of his recurring fits of anger and frenzy, Ivan had killed Ivan Ivanovich, the son who was to have been his heir, striking him with such an angry blow from his hand that he accidentally murdered the young man. The remaining son, Fedor I, who reigned from 1584 to 1598, was unable to rule without help because he was nothing more than "pious, incompetent, perhaps even weak-minded."[58] In his place, the real ruler of Russia was his brother-in-law, Boris Godunov. Though Godunov was cunning, sometimes even conniving, he was more than fit to rule and did so from behind the scenes. On behalf of Fedor, trade throughout Russia was encouraged and expanded, bringing more river traffic and business to the Volga and its tributaries. Moscow gained in importance, a government building program was enacted, and fortifications against possible invaders—including Russia's perennial enemies, the Tatars, as well as the Poles and the Swedes—were erected.

Godunov gained notoriety when, in 1591, nine-year-old Dmitry, a son of Ivan IV's who lived with his mother (Ivan's

After Ivan IV's death in 1584, Boris Godunov served as regent for Ivan's son, Fedor I, and was the defacto leader of Russia. During his official reign as tsar from 1598 to 1605, Godunov helped expand Russia's trade, instituted a government building program, and led a successful war against Sweden.

seventh wife) in Uglich, on the Upper Volga, had his throat slit. Ivan had bequeathed Uglich to Dmitry in his will. The official story was that Dmitry had fallen on a knife he had been playing with just before he experienced an epileptic seizure, but many Russians did not believe the tale, knowing that Godunov would do anything to secure the throne for himself after Fedor's death. Godunov's involvement in Dmitry's death was never proven. It should be noted, however, that during the 14 years Fedor occupied the throne, Godunov "had ample opportunity to usurp the throne, but he devoted himself to the service of the tsar and the nation."[59]

Seven year later, when Fedor died, Godunov was asked to take the throne because there was no clear heir. For seven years, Godunov ruled as tsar, although stories about his involvement in Dmitry's death constantly circulated. For 15 years after Fedor's death, Russia experienced a time of political upheaval and civil conflict, often called "The Time of Troubles" by historians. Godunov ruled until he died of a heart attack in 1605. His son, Fedor Godunov, came to the throne but was murdered after only six months as tsar, assassinated by Godunov's political rivals. At that time, a young man came forward claiming to be the son of Ivan IV, the Dmitry who had died under mysterious circumstances. (Even Dmitry's mother, on being introduced to the claimant to the Russian throne, stated that he was her son.) This "False Dmitry" ruled until he was murdered at the hands of palace guards.

During these years of civil disturbances and political upheaval, the Volga witnessed extensive immigration to its banks. After Ivan IV had conquered the cities of Kazan and Astrakhan along the Volga, he had begun encouraging settlement to the newly opened lands along the Lower and Middle Volga. Frontier settlements sprang up along the great river; these included Kuybyshev, Saratov, and Tsaritsyn, which was destined to become one of the most important on the river, an early incarnation of the modern-day city of Volgograd, also formerly known as Stalingrad. So many peasants had answered the call for immigration to the Volga that Tsar Fedor, through Boris Godunov, had cut off all official migration to these new lands in 1587. Despite the closing of the settlement region and the threat to new settlers of state arrest and physical torture, there was no stopping "the mass flight of thousands upon thousands of desperate peasants during the 'Time of Troubles.' " [60]

During these years of political turmoil in Russia, the people of the kingdom suffered greatly. The government became so weak and ineffective that the Poles were able to invade Russia and even capture Moscow, installing themselves in the Kremlin. During their few years of control over Russia, the Poles were responsible for having the Russian patriarch of the Orthodox Church, the official church of Russia, starved to death. A time of bitter war and revolt among the Russians began, further destroying the social and political fabric of the tsarist empire.

When the bloody period of the Time of Troubles played itself out, Michael Romanov, who was related to Ivan IV's first wife, Anastasia (perhaps the only one of his seven wives whom he truly loved), was selected as the new tsar. The Romanovs had been longtime political rivals of Boris Godunov and other political officials. Michael was only a young man in his teens when he came to power in 1613. He had not been in line for the throne, but the Russian aristocracy agreed to his ascension as tsar as a compromise candidate, one acceptable to the majority of Russian aristocrats, peasants, and the Cossacks, the wildly independent horsemen who ruled much of the rural countryside. With his rise to power, Michael was the first in a line of Russian rulers known as the Romanovs, who would rule the vast Russian state for the next 300 years.

TSAR PETER THE GREAT

During the reigns of the first three Romanov tsars, life for many in Russia—specifically in the Volga region—did not improve much. For all practical purposes, Russia remained a medieval state, with serfdom and land ownership at its economic center. The well-being of the people was generally neglected, and much of the nation's treasury was spent on the needs of the military and on the lavishness of tsarist courts. The greatest step forward for Russia, its people, and its place among the rest of Europe, where significant modernization was occurring, took place during the reign of Peter I, from 1682 to 1725. He became known as Peter the Great.

Peter the Great was a giant of a man, standing nearly seven feet tall; he was physically powerful, undereducated, coarse, and extremely energetic. Although he was tsar, he lived austerely, refusing many of the typical trappings and pomp of the Russian court. It became important to Peter early in his reign that he work hard to bring Russia out of the Middle Ages and into the modern world. He wanted more than anything to make his state like the more advanced western European powers such as France, England, and Holland. Peter took long trips to these countries and others to see how they differed from Russia. (He even went incognito, disguising himself as a minor Russian official and taking jobs in shipyards and carpentry shops.) He went so far in his efforts to modernize that he moved the Russian capital from the eastern locale of Moscow to a more western-oriented site on the Neva River, his "window to the West," a grand, modern city he called St. Petersburg, which developed into an outlet to the Baltic Sea.

Peter realized that to help pay for his modernization programs he would need to generate more revenue from taxes. Because much of the tax burden fell to the peasants and other poor Russians, some of these people tried to escape from their land and move to remote corners of the country. As thousands had

(continued on page 70)

STENKA RAZIN: PIRATE OF THE VOLGA

The Romanov family laid claim to the Russian tsarist throne for 300 years, but they were not always popular leaders. During the years of leadership under the first three Romanovs, beginning with Michael in 1613, thousands of Russian peasants became burdened by the heavy taxes placed on them. As discontent spread across the land, the peasants looked for revolutionary leaders who could help them in their struggles. One of those leaders was a Cossack named Stenka Razin. His story is both fascinating and tragic.

In the midst of the Time of Troubles, great famines spread across Russia, leading to a flight of thousands—who were desperately seeking better lives—to the region of the Volga. The primary impetus for this massive migration was the heavy tax burden placed on them. Because taxes were based on the amount of land a rural farmer had under cultivation, the peasants and small landowners farmed less land, causing a drop in tax revenues for local rulers and the tsars, as well.

In 1649, the second Romanov, Michael's son Alexis, developed a solution to the problem of decreasing tax revenues. He ordered a new set of laws known as the *Ulozhenie*. This law code officially divided all Russians into various classes. Under these laws, the majority of Russia's peasants became serfs—farming servants—bound to an aristocrat whom they were required to serve by working his fields and farms. Others, such as tradesmen, craftsmen, artisans, and traders were required to remain in their own towns, banned from migrating wherever they might choose.

These laws were extremely restrictive and immediately unpopular with many of Russia's poorer populace. For years to follow, rebellions were common, especially along the Lower Volga, where "a strange collection of 'refugees' and adventurers became neighbors in the sparsely settled Volga frontier regions."* Peasant farmers joined forces with the poor scattered remnants of former Tatar tribesmen and Cossacks, who usually cooperated with no one and were driven by a wild spirit of independence. Together, they fought local rulers who to many represented the will of the harsh Romanov tsars.

By the early 1660s, one Cossack began making a name for himself as a revolutionary challenger to aristocratic authority: Stenka Razin. Little is known of Razin's earlier years, but by 1661, his reputation was already spreading. By the late 1660s, the fiery Cossack was leading a band of robber pirates, sailing along the Lower Volga and in the Caspian Sea, and capturing Russian and Persian ships at will. From the mast of his own ship, Razin flew a red flag and a dog's skull "as a pledge that he would bite the Moscovite [aristocrats]."** He and his men boldly struck at defenseless sea towns, such as Derbent, and burned them. In 1670, Razin and a following of 7,000 men sailed up the Don River to the Volga and attacked the settlement town of Tsaritsyn. His next target was Astrakhan, where he "murdered, robbed churches, looted stores."*** As he rampaged and pillaged the Volga countryside, he rallied all Russians who felt oppressed to join him. Gaining followers as he went, Razin next attacked Saratov and Samara. Before the year's end, he was in control of the entire region of the Lower Volga River.

Who was Stenka Razin? Some saw him as the voice of the oppressed; one whose efforts were directed against the rich landowners. Others saw him as nothing more than a river pirate. With each fiery exploit, however, the legend of Razin spread. Poems and songs were written in honor of his deeds and his exploits. The words of one song proclaimed:

> From the white island
> On Mother Volga
> Stenka Razin's brethren
> Sail with a merry song—
>
> Stenka Razin our Father
> The Devil our admiral—
> Sing a song, princess,
> For we are merry today.[†]

Some believed that Razin could not be defeated; that he was so powerful he could not be killed. Such superstitious fantasies were proved to be false when, in 1671, in a battle with government forces outside the town of Simbirsk, Razin was betrayed by wealthy Cossacks and captured. Taken to Moscow, he was tortured and executed. For a century after his death, no one rose up to lead a Russian rebellion with the success of the Cossack pirate Stenka Razin.[†]

* Hall, *Volga*, 41.
** Lamb, *March of Muscovy*, 260.
*** Hall, *Volga*, 42.
[†] Lamb, *March of Muscovy*, 260.

(continued from page 67)

done during the Time of Troubles a century earlier, many fled to the region of the Volga. Throughout Peter's lengthy reign (nearly 40 years), immigrants poured into the Upper Volga region, even though the tsar enacted severe punishments on all those who were caught.

After his death in 1725, Peter the Great was followed as ruler of Russia in rapid order by his widow, Catherine I, who had grown up a peasant; his grandson, Peter II, who died of smallpox; and Anna, a niece, the daughter of his half-brother, Ivan V. Anna appointed a grandnephew, who would have been Ivan VI, to succeed her. That plan was derailed when Elizabeth, a daughter of Peter the Great and Catherine, took the throne for herself and ordered the young Ivan "hidden away in a secret cell in a fortress for the rest of his life."[61] Elizabeth then selected a German nephew, a mentally handicapped, immature young man whom she renamed Peter III, as her heir. She married Peter off to another German, a 15-year-old princess named Sophia of Anhalt-Zerbst. The young German aristocrat arrived in St. Petersburg enthusiastic about the prospects of marrying a future tsar. Taking to her new life in Russia, Sophia converted to the Russian Orthodox Church (she had been raised Lutheran), learned the Russian language, and tried to appeal to the young, dull-witted Peter. The heir to the tsarist throne was so immature, however, that he was still playing with paper dolls and toy soldiers in his early 20s. He also did not care for Sophia, who adopted a Russian name, Catherine.

When Peter inherited the throne, he snubbed Catherine and even spoke of divorcing her, which would have destroyed her future as a royal personage. Peter himself was so unpopular as a ruler (he remained very German and never accepted Russian ways), however, that a plot to assassinate him, which involved members of the military and members of the Russian court, soon developed. The Russian public loved Catherine, however: As one French ambassador noted, "more and more she captures the hearts of the Russians."[62] Peter was murdered, and although Catherine was probably aware of a plot to kill her husband, she probably was not directly involved in the conspiracy.

Although she was just 33 years old when she rose to the throne in 1762, the young German princess, who became the Tsarina Catherine II, was a 20-year veteran of Russian court intrigue and politics. As she took power over the Russian people, her popularity appeared to have no bounds. In a letter, she wrote: "It is impossible to describe to you the joy which the masses of the people show here on seeing me. I have only to make an appearance or to show myself at a window and the cheers are renewed."[63]

TSARINA CATHERINE THE GREAT

Catherine II, who became known as Catherine the Great, retained ties to her native German state and to the German people in general, despite being a favorite of her adopted subjects. During her reign of nearly 35 years, she invited Germans to immigrate to Russia, granting them land in the underpopulated region to the south. There were other official incentives as well: "The immigrants were promised permission to settle where they wished, freedom of religion, a thirty-year tax holiday, perpetual exemption from military service, interest-free loans for ten years for equipment and tools. . . . They were to be given free transportation from Germany to their destinations, living allowances, and more."[64] Although this policy served Catherine well, it was unnecessary. Russia had no need to import colonists from various German states: There "were thousands of Russian people who would have liked the chance to move into the Volga, Don, and Dnieper River valleys."[65]

Between 1762 and 1766, tens of thousands of Germans immigrated to southern Russia, recruited ignorantly by Russian agents who often employed "deceptive and totally misleading descriptions of the settlement area awaiting them."[66] Many

Catherine II, or Catherine the Great, ruled Russia from 1762 to 1796 and continued the modernization programs of Peter the Great. Under Catherine, Russia also expanded its territory, annexing Crimea in 1783 and the eastern provinces of Poland in 1793.

settled along the Middle and Lower Volga. The trip they made from their German homelands to Russian soil often mirrored that of fellow immigrants:

> From St. Petersburg, through which all the immigrants had to pass, the contingents were rafted up the 45-mile Neva [River] to Lake Ladoga and thence to the mouth of the Volkhov river. They then coursed southward up this 130-mile stream into Lake Ilmen. From here most of the parties portaged 200 miles or more to the navigable headwaters of the Volga, down which they then floated and sailed more than 1,100 meandering miles to their distant destination: Saratov. . . . the pioneers had to spend the five- to six-month winters housed with natives in Russian villages along the river. There were alternate routes, but eventually most of them connected somewhere with the Volga. Generally a contingent was en route an entire year from the time of enrollment in Germany.[67]

Other German settlements were established in the Middle Volga region, with a high concentration in and around Saratov and other towns in close proximity. These German emigrants remained so close together, bound by similar experience, language, and customs, that, by the early twentieth century, their descendents who lived along this densely colonized portion of the Volga were recognized by the new Soviet government—which overthrew Tsar Nicholas II, the last of the Russian tsars, in 1917—as the Volga German Autonomous Soviet Socialist Republic. During World War II, when Germany and the U.S.S.R. went to war with one another, the Soviet Communist government rounded up many of the Volga Germans, removed them from their homes, and deported them. By then, more than 750,000 Germans were living in the Soviet Union, approximately half still along the Lower Volga.

THE LAST OF THE RUSSIAN TSARS

After the reign of Catherine the Great, the ties between Russian and German royalty continued through the next century and into the twentieth. Catherine II's son, Paul, reigned from 1796 to 1801 and was assassinated as his father had been. He was followed by his son, Alexander I, who ruled from 1801 to 1825. Alexander's death came early, as well, the result of either suicide or murder on a trip to southern Russia and the region of the Lower Volga. Nicholas I, Alexander's brother, rose to the throne and reigned for three decades. His son, Alexander II, was a popular tsar who "showed greater concern for the well-being of his subjects than any other nineteenth-century tsar had shown."[68] In a bold, sweeping move, Alexander ordered the liberation of Russia's 50 million serfs in 1861. Despite being more enlightened than many of the preceding tsars, Tsar Alexander II had enemies, which included Russian radicals and socialists who plotted his assassination and managed to kill him with a bomb in 1881. (For additional information on this important reformer, enter "Tsar Alexander II" into any search engine and browse the many sites listed.)

Such radicalism also plagued the reign of Alexander II's son, Alexander III. A radical group attempted to kill him, but the plot failed, and five university students were arrested and executed for the murder attempt. One of the five was named Alexander Ulyanov. The conspirator's family was disgraced by the political extremism of the young man, but his younger brother would one day help bring an end to the rule of the Romanovs. Vladimir Ilyich Ulyanov later changed his name to V.I. Lenin and became the father of Russian Communism and the founder of the Soviet state.

Young Lenin grew up along the banks of the Volga. His family owned land at Samara. Despite his older brother's radical political beliefs, Lenin was admitted as a student at the University of Kazan. However, he was expelled within months for taking up the cause of his martyred brother and calling for the violent overthrow of the tsarist government. Returning to Samara, Lenin studied on his own and became more certain of the virtues of socialism and the need for radical change in Russia. Over the coming years, he attended the University of St. Petersburg, passed his law exams, and returned to Samara to practice law. His continuing radicalism resulted in his exile to Siberia in 1897.

Just three years earlier, a new tsar had come to the throne. Nicholas II, the son of Alexander III, was the last of the Romanov line to rule Russia. During his reign, the Russian economy failed to thrive, and Nicholas did little to improve the lives of the common people. He was sometimes as harsh as many of the tsars had been before him. Radical groups grew in number, even if they could not agree on how to protest Nicholas' rule. In 1903, Communist radicals, many from Russia, met in London to discuss their goals. When they could not come to a consensus, they split into two groups, the Bolsheviks and the Mensheviks. Lenin was a part of these socialist discussions (after a few years in Siberian exile, he was allowed to leave Russia), and he had never given up his radicalism. At the conference, he gained control of the Bolshevik faction. It was with this radical organization that Nicholas II would soon find himself locked in a struggle.

During the next decade, the tsar promised the people that he would make political changes, especially after a short-lived revolution in 1905. He made few changes, however, and fought against an expansion of civil liberties in Russia. Radicalism spread throughout the land. Then, in 1914, Russia entered into a great military conflict with other European powers. The Great War (referred to today as World War I) proved extremely difficult for Russia and for Nicholas II. Millions of Russians lost their lives, the economy collapsed, and popular support for the royal house of Romanov reached a crisis in 1917, when

Vladimir Ilyich Ulyanov, or V.I. Lenin, was the leader of the Russian Bolshevik Party, which overthrew Tsar Nicholas II in 1917 and ushered in a more-than-seventy-year period of Communist rule in Russia. This statue of Lenin stands near his tomb in Moscow.

the Bolsheviks rallied against Nicholas, leading to his abdication before year's end. (A year later, the former tsar, his wife, and all five of their children were executed by Bolshevik gunmen.) The Bolshevik Revolution brought Lenin to power as Communism replaced royal government in Russia.

STARVATION AND SALVATION ALONG THE VOLGA

The Bolshevik Revolution brought an end to royal leadership in Russia, but it led the Russian people into years of bitter fighting and civil war. While the war between the Red and White Russians devastated the landscape and killed thousands of people, tens of thousands of residents along the Volga were suffering through another national disaster: famine.

Poor harvests had plagued the Russian people in the past, resulting in the starvation deaths of millions. A Volga-based famine had struck in 1873. The Volga region experienced famine between 1891 and 1892 because of lack of rainfall during the summers, which resulted in poor crop harvests, followed by an extremely harsh winter. The same region faced a famine between 1921 and 1922. Prior to the famine, millions of Russian peasant farmers and others had lost their lives during the fighting in World War I. So many farmers had died that, by 1921, the amount of acreage under cultivation throughout the Volga region was reduced by one-fourth from previous years. As the autumn harvest approached that year, it became clear to millions of people living along the Volga that food would be in extremely short supply.

Complicating the food shortages was the lack of ship transports capable of delivering food to starving residents. Prior to World War I, one-third of Russia's freight goods was transported on the country's rivers and canals, including the Volga. Because of the war and the Russian Revolution, the number of oceangoing ships had been cut in half, from 4,000 to 2,000. Where 25,000 river barges had plied the interior waters of Russia, only 5,500 remained. In 1922, many international groups and governments offered to help deliver food. Heading the relief mission was the American Relief Administration, which had been established by President Warren G. Harding and was administered by an American mining engineer and self-made millionaire, Herbert Hoover.

Americans contributed $25 million to the relief organization, and this money was used to help deliver half a million tons of American food, clothing, and medical supplies across the Atlantic Ocean to the interior of Russia. To aid in the delivery of these emergency supplies, the Russians called for every available boat and rivercraft to be used. Some boat captains arrived from as far as 1,000 miles away. Some of the foodstuffs were delivered to the peasants by wagon, train, and even sled. American grain reached the town of Ulyanovsk, Lenin's hometown, where "more than three thousand horses and sleds had come together, from hundreds of little villages."* That spring, American corn was delivered to the Volga community of Saratov, where "at the sight of the corn, men and women dropped to their knees and gave thanks as Easter bells pealed from Russian churches."** So much food was delivered into the interior of Russia that, by 1923, the threat of famine had largely passed.

* Hall, *Volga*, 70.
** Ibid.

The transfer of power was not smooth: Civil war broke out between the Bolsheviks and their Red Army forces and the Whites, a coalition of "incoherent groups of former officials, nobles, military men, Westernized liberals, and moderate socialists." [69] As civil war raged across Russia, some of the fiercest fighting took place in cities along the Volga. By the early 1920s, Lenin had led the Russian people through the revolution and a new state government—the Union of Soviet Socialist Republics—was established.

Lenin suffered a stroke in 1922, and his personal leadership of the revolution declined dramatically until his death in 1924. In the wake of Lenin's fall from power, the leadership of the Communist Party was in doubt, but Joseph Stalin, a 46-year-old Communist Party boss, came to the forefront espousing a policy of "Socialism in One Country." With the establishment of Russian Communism over the Soviet Union, the future of the Russian Federation and of life along the Volga River would never be the same.

7

War along the Volga

By the early 1930s, the government of Soviet Russia was firmly in place despite the challenges and hardships the people had suffered during the previous decade. All was not well at home, however, and economic problems continued to plague the Stalinist state. The Soviet Union was soon facing a new challenge, the threat of a newly organized German state under the political leadership of fascist dictator Adolf Hitler. By 1934, Hitler's power over Germany was consolidated, giving him and his political supporters, the National Socialist German Workers Party, known popularly as the Nazi Party, free rein over the German people in every aspect of their lives—economic, political, and social.

Hitler and his followers were rabidly anti-Communist and were violently opposed to the existence of the Soviet state. The Nazis banned Communism from Germany, produced extensive propaganda in support of all anti-Soviet forces across Europe, and abandoned any political ties with the Soviet Union as quickly as possible. The Soviet leadership was so concerned about Hitler's intentions in Europe that it supported joining the League of Nations, which Stalin and others had always criticized. When the Soviets asked Hitler to guarantee the continued independence of the Baltic states of Lithuania, Latvia, and Estonia, which Stalin considered essential to Soviet security, the German leader rejected the request. The Soviet government began extending no-aggression agreements already in place with Poland, Latvia, Estonia, and Finland. Eastern European states that had kept the Soviet Union at arm's length out of fear soon began to diplomatically recognize the Communist government. By 1935, a great political gulf between Nazi Germany and the Soviet Union existed.

During the late 1930s, as Hitler's military began to systematically attack or simply annex Germany's closest neighbors, such as Austria and Czechoslovakia, the Soviet Union began

Despite signing a nonaggression treaty—the Molotov-Ribbentrop Pact—with the Soviet Union in August 1939, Nazi Germany invaded Poland on September 1, 1939 (troops are shown here marching down a Polish street). Faced with the threat of the Wehrmacht, or German war machine, on its doorstep, the Soviet Union took countermeasures by invading eastern Poland and Finland to create a buffer zone between themselves and Germany.

negotiations with the leaders of France and Great Britain (Russia's allies during World War I) to establish military alliances. The talks failed, however, and the desperate Soviet leadership signed a nonaggression pact with Germany, instead, in August 1939. The agreement did not deter Hitler's aggressiveness toward other countries, however: On September 1, the Germans invaded Poland. The move was alarming to Stalin because both the Soviets and the Germans shared borders with Poland. In response, the Soviet military was ordered into eastern Poland as a countersecurity measure. Within weeks, the Nazis and the Communists carved Polish territory in two.

Once the Soviets had taken the offensive in Poland, they took additional steps to establish a greater region of security. In November 1939, the Soviets invaded Finland to create a new buffer state between Germany and Russia.

Then, during the spring of 1940, the Russians were given a reprieve when Hitler launched a series of military invasions not toward the Soviet Union but into western Europe. Between May and June, the German Wehrmacht invaded and took control of Norway, Denmark, Luxembourg, Holland, and Belgium. Hitler's *blitzkrieg*—lightning war—soon caused the unthinkable: the fall of France. The western campaigns of Hitler's Wehrmacht only gave the Soviet Union a brief respite. In fact, Hitler was so ecstatic about his military successes against western Europe that he became determined to launch an offensive into the east—against the Soviet Union.

As Hitler busied himself and his commanders with the plans for an invasion of the Soviet Union, the Soviet leadership was also taking bold steps. During the summer of 1940, Stalin ordered the annexation of the Baltic states of Lithuania, Latvia, and Estonia, as well as Bessarabia, which was wrested from Romanian control. Step by step, the Soviets and the Germans were coming closer and closer to one another. A showdown between the two major European powers was nearing with each passing month.

By December, Hitler had finalized his plans for the invasion of the Soviet Union. The German military command had assembled a military force of gigantic proportions to step onto Soviet soil with an invasion plan called Operation Barbarossa. The Germans intended to commit 3 million troops—a total of 148 divisions or 80 percent of the German army. Thousands of Luftwaffe planes, as well as 6,000 artillery pieces, were earmarked for the operation. Nineteen tank divisions, totaling 2,400 tanks, were to participate in the invasion. Fourteen motorized infantry divisions, representing the centerpiece of Hitler's war machine and which had already bowled over enemies from Czechoslovakia to France and Norway to Poland, were put on alert.

Hitler's plan called for a three-pronged attack against the Soviet Union. One prong was to advance on the northern city of Leningrad, and a second was to advance across Ukraine and Belarus and attack the cities of Minsk, Smolensk, and their key target, Moscow. The third element of Hitler's attack group was to roll across southern Poland, Hungary, and Romania into southern Russia and Ukraine. Although Hitler's plans for invasion set May 1941 as the target date for the attack, German tanks and planes did not move against the Soviet Union until June 22. (A bogged-down offensive in the Balkans, including Yugoslavia, caused the delay.)

When the invasion did commence, the Soviets were sent reeling back. It was not as though the Russians had not seen the attack coming. The Soviet High Command had established a lengthy defensive line along the Soviet border; it included 170 divisions divided into two immense battle groups. The Soviets made mistakes in preparation, however: "They had ignored Western warnings and did not expect such an early, sudden, and powerful offensive."[70] Stalin had attempted to prepare for the massive German assault, but he and his commanders had failed to anticipate the intensity of Hitler's blitzkrieg. The result was the wholesale destruction of Russia's defenses:

> Although it encountered some determined resistance, the German war machine rolled inexorably along the entire front, particularly in three directions: in the north against Leningrad, in the center towards Moscow, and in the south towards Kiev and Rostov-on-Don. Entire Soviet armies were smashed and taken prisoner at Bialystok, Minsk, and Kiev, which fell in September. The southern wing of the invasion swept across the Ukraine.[71]

Despite a successful invasion of the Soviet Union, not every aspect of the Nazi leader's grand plan fell into place. His advance against Leningrad resulted in a siege that stretched on for two and a half years. The brave people of the city held out but starvation reduced their numbers dramatically. When the siege began, Leningrad was a metropolis of 4 million residents. When the siege was finally broken, the city's population had been reduced by 1.5 million. The remaining beleaguered citizenry had survived by eating every animal, including their personal pets, and making soup of dried wallpaper glue and boiled leather attaché cases and suitcases. The siege ended with the German failure to bring down this important Soviet city.

The main German blow, the assault on Moscow, was delayed by intense fighting around Smolensk. Unable to reach the Soviet capital until the fall of 1941, Hitler's "summer Blitzkrieg became a fall campaign."[72] After additional German divisions were added to the Moscow advance, bringing the total to 240, the Wehrmacht finally broke through Soviet resistance in October, coming to within 60 miles of the city. In a panic, Stalin and his government abandoned Moscow and made a

Soviet soldiers (shown here) enjoyed a significant advantage over their German counterparts in that they were better prepared to face the bitter cold Russian winters during Germany's invasion of the Soviet Union during World War II. The German High Command did not issue winter clothing to its troops, and the fighters in the field suffered greatly. German soldiers were decimated by both the freezing temperatures and the Soviet counteroffensive during the winter of 1941–1942, which resulted in some 750,000 German casualties.

break for Kuybyshev, the city on the Volga formerly known as Samara. Autumn rains slowed the German advance, however, as did a tenacious defense by Moscow's protectors, keeping the Nazis 20 miles from the Soviet city.

Then, a harsh Russian winter set in, locking the Germans in their tank tracks. The German High Command had failed to issue winter clothing to its troops, and the fighters in the field suffered greatly. Temperatures fell to below zero, and frostbite took its toll on the Nazis, afflicting 100,000 German soldiers and causing 2,000 amputations. Through the winter of 1941–1942, Hitler's forces failed to bring about the fall of two major Soviet cities and experienced 750,000 casualties, including 200,000 troops killed. A Russian counteroffensive commenced in December 1941, and, facing 100 Russian divisions, the Wehrmacht fell apart. Thousands of German soldiers were taken prisoner, some captured "wearing women's furs and silk underclothing to supplement their inadequate uniforms against the cold."[73]

The failure to capture the Soviet capital did not deter Hitler, despite the fact that his forces had faced staggering losses during a single winter battling on the frozen Russian landscape. By the spring of 1942, the Germans had suffered more than 150,000 casualties, including more than 50,000 dead, during the siege of Moscow alone. Soviet losses had been equally serious:

> Of the 22,000 tanks the Soviets had in service before 1939, only 1,000 were still operational. Every mechanized Soviet corps had been destroyed. A total of 177 Soviet rifle divisions no longer existed. In the defense of Moscow, where the fighting had been extremely intense, Stalin's forces had counted one million casualties. Surrendering Soviet armies had given the Germans 3 million prisoners of war. In the midst of the winter of 1941–42, the Russians could muster only about 250,000 troops to maintain the defense of their Communist nation.[74]

Even though the German war machine had failed to bring Russia to its knees with the 1941–1942 campaigns, Hitler had no intention of giving up on Soviet soil. He altered his timeline drastically, setting new objectives for his struggling German forces. A dire shortage of oil led the German leader to order an assault farther across southern Russia, toward the oil-rich region of the Caucasus Mountains, situated between the Black and Caspian Seas. Oil was what prompted Hitler's next military move across the Soviet landscape, but he also had designs on another Russian city, one that was an important industrial center and was named after his Soviet counterpart—the city of Stalingrad, located along the banks of the Volga River.

"STALIN'S CITY"

A giant showdown occurred between these two European powers in 1942. The Germans launched their offensive early in July, and, by the next month, a German army of 300,000 had crossed the Don River and driven clear to the Volga. By the end of August, the Wehrmacht was closing in on Stalingrad. Massive recruiting during the previous winter had resulted in 900,000 new German troops, all desperately needed to continue Hitler's campaign against Russia and provide man-power for the other theaters of the war. Yet the forces that mobilized on Soviet soil after the spring thaw of 1942 were still fewer than the number that had invaded Russia and Ukraine during the previous summer's campaign. The Russians had desperately scrambled through the winter to increase the number of troops in the Red Army to 9 million. Soviet factories, running around the clock, had cranked out 5,000 new tanks, 14,000 artillery pieces, 50,000 mortars, and 3,000 planes.

Stalingrad, a target Hitler obsessed over, was positioned along the meandering west bank of the Volga River. The city was old, even for Russia, and had experienced earlier invasions, such as the 1237 Mongol incursion at the hands of Batu Khan. By the late sixteenth century, the Russians had estab-lished a trading outpost at this Volga site, called Tsaritsyn, a

Tatar word meaning "yellow water." The 1670 siege led by Stenka Razin had resulted in the capture of the Russian river town. During the late 1800s, with the building of a French steel mill along the Volga, Tsaritsyn was developing as an industrial city. By World War I, Tsaritsyn was one of the most industrialized cities in Russia, a mechanized community where one of every four citizens worked in a factory or in another industry-based job. After Joseph Stalin had helped the Red Army turn away several White Army attacks against Tsaritsyn in 1920, the people of this town renamed their city Stalingrad.

It was its name that drew Hitler to send troops to capture it—that and its manufacturing capacity. Stalingrad was home to giant industrial plants, including the Barrikady gun factory; the Lazur chemical plant; the Red October facility, which was a foundry and machine-tool producing plant; and the Dzerhezinsky Tractor Works, whose main building stretched a mile along the river. During the summer of 1942, Stalingrad "looked like a giant caterpillar, sixteen miles long and filled with smokestacks belching forth clouds of soot that told of its value to the Soviet war effort."[75] The city was preparing for the German advance, one that had nearly destroyed the populations of Leningrad and Moscow the previous year.

By August, German Field Marshal Friedrich von Paulus began to advance his troops toward Stalingrad, and, within a week, Luftwaffe planes were bombing Ostrov just 60 miles from the targeted Volga city. In short order, the German Sixth Army captured more than 50,000 Soviet troops and destroyed 1,000 tanks. Soviet units began to abandon their posts, fleeing into the city. On August 14, the Wehrmacht hit hard against the Soviet Fourth Tank Army and threw it back, a loss resulting in the capture of tens of thousands of Soviet fighters.

Less than 10 days later, the Germans had managed to complete an extraordinary run north of Stalingrad, reaching the Volga town of Rynok. Before the end of the month, three separate but well-coordinated German divisions were bearing down on Stalingrad. The city was nearly surrounded as Field Marshal Paulus became set in his determination to establish a "forty-mile-long corridor from the Don to the Volga."[76] German tanks stood ready to enter Stalingrad.

Within the besieged city, the Soviet military was feverishly rallying the people, calling for everyone who was able to fight. Political commissars and factory bosses gave instructions to the citizenry: "Whoever can bear arms and whoever can shoot, write your names down."[77] Tens of thousands of Stalingrad's civilians did take up arms and contributed to the stiff resistance that frustrated the Germans during the months that followed.

By September, Luftwaffe planes had destroyed much of the cityscape, including its industrial sector. Stalingrad's Red Square and the surrounding 100 blocks were leveled by air bombings. At all times, somewhere in the city, fires blazed until they burned themselves out. The city's waterworks were destroyed early on, making fire fighting impossible.

Stalingrad itself became a battleground. Although the city had no fortifications or permanent defensive structures, the Russians held out for weeks. With support from massive gun emplacements gathered on the opposite bank of the Volga, General Vassili Chuikov's 62nd Army fought tenaciously for every city block, every building, and every individual house and home. Through the months of fighting, the city was reduced to rubble, which ultimately worked to the advantage of the city's defenders. With the streets littered with building debris, giant chunks of concrete, and endless scatterings of brick, it was nearly impossible for the German tanks to maneuver from one part of the city to another.

Throughout the city's factory sector, devastated plant build-ings became the strongholds for defenders as street fighting became commonplace. One German officer described the urban battlefield:

> The street is no longer measured by meters but by corpses.
> . . . We have fought for fifteen days for a single house with
> mortars, grenades, machine-guns and bayonets. . . . There is
> a ceaseless struggle from noon to night. From story to story,
> faces black with sweat, we bombed each other with
> grenades in the middle of explosions, clouds of dust and
> smoke. . . . Stalingrad is no longer a town. By day it is an
> enormous cloud of burning, blinding smoke; it is a vast
> furnace lit by the reflection of the flames.[78]

In this conflict, which both the Germans and Soviets knew could determine the outcome of the war, the Volga River played a significant role in turning the tide of the German onslaught. Soviet reinforcements were brought into the city from the opposite bank of the river, usually crossing at night "to avoid the incessant German bombardment that made daylight trips suicidal."[79] Several crossing sites were utilized but two were highly important: the Skudri Crossing, which served the area north of the tractor plant to Rynok, and Crossing 62, a mooring complex located between the Red October plant and the Barrikady gun factory, both of which were reduced to bombed-out shells. Even at night, the fresh, unseasoned Soviet recruits who made the Volga crossing saw sights that filled them with fear:

> The nightly voyages to Crossings 62 and Skudri were a
> ghastly shock to soldiers joining the battle. The sight of
> the city on fire, the deep rumble of thousands of guns,
> instinctively made them recoil. But Communist party
> agitators, *politrook*, were always with them, working with
> ferocious zeal to calm them down. . . . When men were hit,

screamed, and died, the *politrook* worked harder to keep
the rest of the group from succumbing to mob fear. Sometimes they failed, and soldiers leaped into the Volga. The
politrook emptied their guns into these swimmers.[80]

Despite the dangers of the Volga crossings, by October the
Soviets had delivered 100,000 troops to Stalingrad by way of
the river. Many of them died quickly in the face of stiff German
firepower. By the end of October, General Chuikov's forces still
only numbered close to 50,000. Within just a matter of weeks,
the Soviet 62nd army had experienced 80,000 casualties.

October proved to be the turning point in the raging
battle for Stalingrad. The German fighters had marched
1,500 miles inside the Soviet Union just to reach the gate
of the city, so it was difficult for the Wehrmacht to replace
its losses, whether equipment or men. The Soviets, fighting
on their own soil, were able to feed increasing numbers of
fighters to the front, and Soviet factories, many relocated to
the safety of the Ural Mountains, provided a steady stream
of armament replacements. By November, "the Soviets had
40 percent more tanks and motorized artillery and 30 percent
more field guns and mortars than the Germans had. They
also had 10 percent more planes than the Luftwaffe com-
manded in the Stalingrad region."[81]

As German units pushed the Soviet defenders in the city out
of many of their defensive positions through October and
early November, Russian forces were gathering outside the city,
taking positions along a 200-mile front. During the previous
three months of fighting, Soviet commanders had ordered half
of the Red Army's available reserve of artillery pieces to be
moved into the Stalingrad region to provide firepower for a
Soviet counteroffensive. Four Soviet air force units, including
1,000 new planes, 60 percent of which were much-needed
fighters, were put in place.

On November 19, one million Soviet troops moved forward along the counteroffensive line, intent on surrounding the Germans outside the city. When the Soviets rolled forward, they did not immediately engage German forces but rather engaged Romanians, Italians, and Hungarians—allies of Hitler's troops. The Soviets achieved immediate success. The Russian guns, numbering almost 100 per mile of front, pounded the enemy and cut off the Germans from their allied field support. In less than a week, the Soviets had turned the siege of Stalingrad into a siege of the Germans. By November 23, 300,000 Germans, including Field Marshal Paulus' entire Sixth Army—locked inside Stalingrad—were completely surrounded. Right behind the advancing Soviets roared a wintry blast, as a merciless Russian winter set in. The Germans had stayed too long. Through the following months, they paid a heavy price for failing to bring about the fall of Stalingrad during the warmer autumn months.

The Soviets had brilliantly and desperately turned around the German offensive, and the advantage remained theirs until the surrender of Paulus' forces at the beginning of February 1943. When the German Wehrmacht finally abandoned its mission to destroy Stalingrad, 120,000 German and Romanian troops were left in the city and the surrounding area. The campaign to push the Soviets against the natural barrier of the Volga had failed miserably. The Germans, "who had not quite twice as many men, more weapons and more than twice as many aircraft, eventually lost up to two hundred thousand men and vast quantities of arms, planes and motorized vehicles." [82]

During the German advance, the Russians had heroically taken up arms against the Nazi invaders, rallied by battle cries that included: "The enemy will be halted and defeated. Beyond the Volga there's no land for you!" [83] Indeed, through their tenacious defense of their city, the Soviets had managed

Stalingrad, located on the west bank of the Volga River, was a prime target for Nazi Germany due to the city's large manufacturing capacity. In September 1942, the Germans began to lay siege to the city. Miraculously, the residents of Stalingrad and the Soviet Army were steadfast in their defense of the city, eventually defeating the Germans in February 1943. Shown here are the battered remains of Stalingrad, where total casualties were estimated to have been between 1 and 2 million people.

to keep the Germans from reaching the banks of the Volga. In the entire six months of fighting, the Germans "never crossed the last 200 meter (220 yard) strip between their front line and the river."[84]

The cost on both sides was almost incalculable. During the three months they were trapped in the city, 150,000 Germans and Romanians died. More than 100,000 Axis (those who were allied with the Germans) forces surrendered. The Soviets captured 6,000 German artillery pieces and 60,000 motorized vehicles of war. Stalingrad emerged a bombed-out shell. Between September 1942 and January 1943, "99 percent of the city had been reduced to rubble," [85] including "41,000 homes, 300 factories, and 113 hospitals and schools." [86] When the siege began, half a million people called the city home. When the siege ended, only 1,515 of those residents remained. The others had either fled across the Volga to safety or been killed defending the great city on the Volga. (For additional information on this catastrophic conflict, enter "Battle of Stalingrad" into any search engine and browse the many sites listed.)

8

A Trip Down the Volga

Today, the guns along the Volga that shattered the lives of the people of Stalingrad, as well as much of the western portion of the Soviet Union, have fallen silent. Those with memories of World War II (the Russians refer to the massive conflict as the Great Patriotic War) are mostly gone. Not only has the war been relegated to the pages of history, so has the Soviet Union itself. Through the decades after World War II, Soviet Communism struggled to improve the lives of its citizens, even as the government refused to recognize civil liberties, as well as economic freedom, for its people. By the late 1980s, the Communist-led government began to unravel as harsh economic realities finally brought down the political experiment Lenin and Stalin had established nearly 75 years earlier.

With the fall of the Union of Soviet Socialist Republics and the emergence of a modern, independent Russia, the Volga continues to represent a vital lifeline for the Russian people. The river remains an important trade route into the Russian interior, and thousands of river barges still ply its waters. The Volga is also an important tourist attraction, where millions of Russians take vacation cruises along the river, and, in doing so, are able to reconnect with many of the sites along the grand old Russian waterway that helped form the history of both the river and of Russia itself. Cruise ships operating out of Moscow take the Moscow Canal, which reaches the Upper Volga River southwest of the Rybinsk Reservoir (the water impounded in the reservoir provides the water for the Moscow Canal) or sail down the Oka River, which flows past Moscow, reaching the Volga at the city of Gorky.

All along the river, cities provide visitors with a window into the past while also revealing modern changes. Ships from Moscow reach the Volga at Ivankovo, a little downriver from Tver and formerly known as Kalinin. Kalinin rivaled Moscow as one of Russia's greatest trading communities during the thirteenth, fourteenth, and fifteenth centuries. Today, Tver is known for

A bridge crosses the Volga at Yaroslavl, Russia, which is northeast of Moscow. The city is named for Yaroslav the Wise and is an important industrial center.

its industry, including textile production and the construction of railroad cars. Slightly downriver stands Uglich, where, nearly four centuries ago, Boris Godunov nearly destroyed the peasant village for the role the locals played in plotting against Prince Dmitry during Russia's Time of Troubles.

Modernization and Russian history continue to mix down-river at Rybinsk, where the city is the scene of shipbuilding facilities and wood-processing plants. At Yaroslavl, one of the early settlement sites along the river and named for Yaroslav the Wise, factories including rubber-producing plants dot the banks. A majority of the residents of Yaroslavl work in industry-related jobs. Unfortunately, these industrial plants and hundreds of others along the Volga produce thousands of tons of pollutants annually, much of which is dumped into the river. Regional farming fields also contaminate the Volga with agricultural runoff, including fertilizers and other chemicals. Such pollutants have dramatically affected the vitality of the fish population in the river and have almost been catastrophic to the sturgeon that are the source of some of Russia's legendary caviar.

Farther along lies Kostroma, originally erected as a fort to guard against Tatar invasions. It was here that Michael Romanov, the first of the great line of tsars, was authorized by the Russian nobility to become a royal leader. Where Moscow's Oka River reaches the Volga, Gorky stands in the midst of the heaviest river barge traffic. In the nineteenth and early twentieth centuries, Volga boatmen plied these waters, their trade barges often pulled by teams of men harnessed together and walking along the banks of the river. Today, the modern barges are diesel powered.

In previous centuries, Gorky was a trading center, an international crossroads, known as Novgorod. Here, "Persian, Greek, Turkish, and German dealers worked feverishly selling the products they had brought from their homelands, and gestured wildly as they tried to make themselves understood in a dozen different languages."[87] In 1932, Stalin renamed the city after the great Russian writer Maxim Gorky, but the name was changed to Nizhny Novgorod in 1991.

Twentieth-century modernization had made the Middle Volga one of the most productive and fastest growing regions of the Soviet Union. Oil was discovered between the Volga River and the Ural Mountains in 1929. By 1960, the drilling being done in the Volga-Ural region revealed extensive underground deposits near Volgograd (formerly Stalingrad) and Perm, which sits near the headwaters of the Kama River, one of the Volga's many tributaries. In the decades that followed, most of Russia's oil was tapped from wells drilled in this region. Oil and natural gas deposits have continued to help develop the Middle Volga between Kazan to the north and Volgograd to the south, near where the Don River swings in a wide arc to the east, nearly reaching the west bank of the Volga.

Modernization has also changed the nature of the Volga. The Volga was historically a river of extremes, prone to annual flooding, but it has now largely been tamed, as many rivers around the world have been. A system of dams, spillways, floodgates, and pumping stations line the banks along the full length of the river at sites such as Ivankovo, Uglich, Rybinsk, Gorodets, Kuybyshev, and Volgograd. At each of the dam sites, man-made lakes have developed as water backs up behind the river-control barriers. These dams produce hydroelectric power for much of Russia. When the Lenin Hydroelectric Station came on line at Kuybyshev in 1957, it was the largest electric-producing plant in the world. When the Volgograd Hydroelectric Station began full-capacity operation in 1960, it proved even larger. Here, the Volga River is put to work to provide power for the plant's nearly two dozen turbogenerators.

As cruise ships sail through the Middle Volga, the passengers pass Kazan, built hundreds of years ago as a Tatar city. By the twentieth century, Kazan was home to a university that Lenin attended, as did Leo Tolstoy, the author of notable Russian novels such as *Anna Karenina* and *War and Peace*. Farther along, the town of Ulyanovsk, formerly known as Simbirsk, is remembered as V.I. Lenin's hometown. The city was named after him in 1923. The next city of note along the Volga is Kuybyshev, remembered in history as Samara.

All along the banks of the Volga and stretching for miles into the distance are grain fields, part of the great Russian bread

Saratov, an important Volga port city and terminus for agricultural products in southern Russia, was home to many ethnic Germans who have since been repatriated. Saratov was also one of the cities that Russian Cossack pirate Stenka Razin captured during his pillaging of the Lower Volga region in the late seventeenth century.

basket of the twentieth century. Also dotting this region are factories, mills, and food plants. Fifty miles downriver from Kuybyshev is Syzran, a great oil refining city; then Saratov; and finally Volgograd, where early Russian leaders first built Tsaritsyn. The city has been rebuilt since the war, rising from the ashes of a massive conflict like the mythological phoenix. Today, it is home to 2.7 million people.

As the great river flows toward the Caspian Sea, it reaches Astrakhan, an old Tatar site today known for its fishing industry. Here, thousands of Volga barges and riverboats work the river as thousands have over the centuries. Fishermen harvest some of the greatest caviar in the world from the waters of the Lower Volga. Fish hatcheries have been built along the river to help provide spawning grounds for the sturgeon that produce black caviar. From Astrakhan, the river spreads out wide, fanning in every direction into its delta lowlands, as it flows into the great Caspian Sea.

Throughout Russia's history, as a multitude of people have come and gone, invaded, conquered, settled, harvested, prospered, or struggled, the great Mother Volga has continued to wind its course and deliver its waters to the sea. With the turning of the pages of Russia's past, the Volga is remembered as a river that contributed to the ebb and flow of an immense and powerful state, one that, even today, stands at the crossroads of Europe and Asia. What role will the Volga River play in the future? Perhaps the answer lies in the words of a Russian writer who believes that the river is a continuing and vital contributor to Russia's future: "The Volga seems to me to typify [the] Russian heart, and the Volga will still be there at the end, when the Last History is written."[88]

13000 B.C. Glaciers cover much of the region of northern Europe, including that of the modern-day Volga River and its neighboring rivers and tributaries.

3000 B.C. Early Indo-European peoples migrate to Russian steppes and its rivers, including the Volga River; region of the Volga becomes permanently occupied, as village life replaces nomadism.

2000–1000 B.C. Those living along the steppes and the Volga develop a more complicated lifestyle than their neighbors to the north.

1000 B.C. Aryan group of nomads, the Cimmerians, begin to conquer their neighbors throughout the central region of Russia and the Lower Volga.

700–200 B.C. Scythians reach the Volga region and establish themselves as the center of power.

3000 B.C.
Indo-Europeans arrive at the Volga River

1200
Mongolians known as the "Golden Horde" invade Russian state

1000 B.C.
Cimmerians begin conquering Lower Volga

700s–1100s
The Rus, or Varangians, come from Scandinavia and plunder Volga towns

700–200 B.C.
Scythians rule Volga region

3000 B.C.   *A.D. 200*   *1000*   *1400*

200 B.C.–A.D. 200
Sarmatians conquer Scythians and rule central Russia

800s
East Slavs develop towns along the Volga, including Novgorod, Smolensk, and Kiev

A.D. 200s–300s
The Goths, a Germanic tribe, come from southern Europe to settle Volga region

370
Asiatic Huns drive out Goths and rule territory from the Volga to the Danube

late 1400s
Russian capital moved from Kiev to Moscow

200 B.C.–A.D. 200	Arrival of Sarmatians in central Russia and beginning of four centuries of dominance.
A.D. 200s–300s	Germanic tribes, including the Goths, reach the Volga and establish permanent presence.
370	Asiatic Huns reach the Russian steppes, driving the Goths back across the borders of the Roman Empire.
550	Avars reach the Volga and dominate the region for more than 200 years.
700s	Khazars invade and dominate the Volga region.
700s–1100s	The Scandinavian "Rus" or "Varangians" reach the Volga, becoming infamous for their constant raiding and pillaging of towns, seaports, and monasteries.

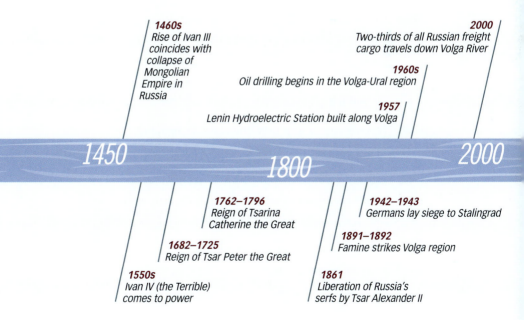

1460s
Rise of Ivan III coincides with collapse of Mongolian Empire in Russia

2000
Two-thirds of all Russian freight cargo travels down Volga River

1960s
Oil drilling begins in the Volga-Ural region

1957
Lenin Hydroelectric Station built along Volga

1450

1800

2000

1762–1796
Reign of Tsarina Catherine the Great

1942–1943
Germans lay siege to Stalingrad

1682–1725
Reign of Tsar Peter the Great

1891–1892
Famine strikes Volga region

1550s
Ivan IV (the Terrible) comes to power

1861
Liberation of Russia's serfs by Tsar Alexander II

800s   East Slavs' presence in Russia develops, including permanent settlements and involved economic systems; they establish important towns and villages within the region of the Volga, including Novgorod, Smolensk, and Kiev.

1100–1400   Era of Kievan Russia; Russian princes rule the Volga region and establish Kiev as their headquarters.

1200s   Invasions into the Volga region by eastern raiders known as the Mongolian "Golden Horde."

1237   Mongolian invasion and destruction of the Volga region city of Riazan.

1370s   Grand Duke of Moscow, Dimitri, rallies the Russian people against the ruling khan, Mamai.

EARLY 1400s   The rule of the Golden Horde begins to steadily decline; by mid-1400s, the Mongolian influence is broken in the Volga region.

1460s   Collapse of the Mongolian Empire in Russia coincides with the rise of an aristocratic Russian leader, Ivan III (1462–1505); during his reign, Ivan establishes Moscow, in the Upper Volga region, as his capital.

1550s   Ivan IV comes to power and extends the lands under the control of the Russian leadership.

EARLY 1600s   At the encouragement of Ivan IV, frontier settlements spring up along the Volga River, especially the river's lower and middle courses.

1660s   Volga-based robber-pirate, Stenka Razin, actively terrorizes towns and settlements along the river.

1682–1725 Reign of Tsar Peter the Great; during his reign, immigrants pour into the frontier Upper Volga region, many to escape the harsh tax burden imposed by Peter.

1762–1796 Tens of thousands of Germans immigrate to southern Russia during the reign of Tsarina Catherine II, who was of German descent.

1825 Tsar Alexander I dies, either by suicide or murder, while on a trip to southern Russia and the region of the Lower Volga.

1861 Tsar Alexander II liberates Russia's 50 million serfs, many of whom live within the region of the Volga.

1873 Volga-based famine strikes the region due to poor grain harvests.

1891–92 Famine strikes the Volga region due to poor rainfall, poor harvests, and a harsh winter.

1921–22 Volga region experiences another severe famine, due to a drastic drop in agricultural production caused by the deaths of so many Russian peasant farmers during World War I; in 1922, American Relief Administration sends half a million tons of food to Russia.

1941 German Nazis invade the Soviet Union, including the Volga region.

1942–1943 Germans lay siege to the Volga city of Stalingrad from August to February; siege is finally broken by the Russian Army, though the city is completely reduced to rubble.

1940s 750,000 Germans living along the Lower Volga are removed from their homes and deported by the Stalinist government.

1957 Lenin Hydroelectric Station, built on the Volga, comes on line as the largest electric-producing plant in the world.

1960s Oil drilling begins in the Volga-Ural region, uncovering extensive deposits of petroleum.

2000 Volga River carries two-thirds of all Russian freight cargo; half of the country's farmers live on or near the Volga.

CHAPTER 1:
A Nation's Great River

1 Ian Grey, *The Horizon History of Russia* (New York: American Heritage Publishing Co., 1970), 15.

2 Ibid.

CHAPTER 2:
Early People of the Volga

3 Jesse D. Clarkson, *A History of Russia* (New York: Random House, 1961), 12.

4 Ibid., 13.

5 Ibid.

6 Nicholas V. Riasanovsky, *A History of Russia* (New York: Oxford University Press, 1963), 14.

7 Ibid., 15.

8 Clarkson, *History of Russia*, 14.

9 Grey, *Horizon History*, 17.

10 Riasanovsky, *History of Russia*, 17.

11 Clarkson, *History of Russia*, 14.

12 Riasanovsky, *History of Russia*, 17.

13 Clarkson, *History of Russia*, 15.

14 Riasanovsky, *History of Russia*, 17.

15 Grey, *Horizon History*, 17.

16 Ibid., 19.

17 Riasanovsky, *History of Russia*, 20.

CHAPTER 3:
The Rus

18 *What Life Was Like When Longships Sailed: Vikings, A.D. 800–1100* (Alexandria, Va: Time-Life Books, 1998), 40.

19 Grey, *Horizon History*, 20.

20 Ibid., 24.

21 Ibid.

22 Walther Kirchner, *A History of Russia* (New York: Barnes & Noble, 1955), 8–9.

23 Ibid., 9.

24 Clarkson, *History of Russia*, 30.

25 Ibid.

26 James Graham-Campbell, ed., *Cultural Atlas of the Viking World* (New York: Facts on File, Inc., 1994), 198.

27 Magnus Magnusson, *Vikings!* (New York: E.P. Dutton, 1980), 107–108.

28 Graham-Campbell, *Cultural Atlas*, 197.

29 Ibid., 198.

30 Ibid.

31 Ibid.

32 Kirchner, *History of Russia*, 21.

33 Ibid., 22.

34 Ibid., 23.

CHAPTER 4:
The Golden Horde

35 Riasanovsky, *History of Russia*, 73.

36 Ibid.

37 Ibid., 75.

38 Grey, *Horizon History*, 44.

39 Ibid., 45.

40 Ibid., 46.

41 Ibid.

42 Ibid.

43 Ibid., 47.

44 Michael T. Florinsky, *Russia: A History and Interpretation*, vol. 1 (New York: Macmillan Company, 1947), 79.

45 Grey, *Horizon History*, 48

46 Ibid., 56.

47 Riasanovsky, *History of Russia*, 81.

48 *When Longships Sailed*, 58.

CHAPTER 5:
The Rise of the Tsars

49 Harold Lamb, *The March of Muscovy: Ivan the Terrible and the Growth of the Russian Empire, 1400–1648* (Garden City, N.Y.: Doubleday & Company, 1948), 92.

50 Ibid., 101.

51 Ibid., 105.

52 bid.

53 Ibid.

54 Ibid.

55 Elvajean Hall, *The Volga: Lifeline of Russia* (Chicago, Ill.: Rand McNally Company, 1965), 31.

56 Grey, *Horizon History*, 94.

57 Ibid.

CHAPTER 6:
Modernization along the Volga

58 Kirchner, *History of Russia*, 53.

59 Ibid., 54.

60 Hall, *Volga*, 36.

61 Ibid., 46.

62 Grey, *Horizon History*, 197.

63 Ibid., 199.

64 Marq DeVilliers, *Down the Volga: A Journey through Mother Russia in a Time of Troubles* (New York: Viking Press, 1991), 252.

65 Hall, *Volga*, 47.

66 Fred Koch and Jacob Eichhorn, *The Volga Germans: in Russia and the Americas, from 1763 to the Present* (University Park, Pa.: The Pennsylvania State University Press, 1977), 8.

67 Ibid., 20.

68 Hall, *Volga*, 52.

69 Kirchner, *History of Russia*, 217.

CHAPTER 7:
War along the Volga

70 Riasanovsky, *History of Russia*, 574.

71 Ibid.

72 Ibid.

73 Stephen Ambrose, *American Heritage New History of World War II* (New York: Viking, 1997), 39.

74 Tim McNeese, *Stalingrad* (Philadelphia, Pa.: Chelsea House Publishers, 2003), 40.

75 William Craig, *Enemy at the Gates: The Battle for Stalingrad* (Old Saybrook, Conn.: Konecky & Konecky, 1973), 29.

76 Ibid., 63.

77 Ibid., 56.

78 Ambrose, *New History*, 247.

79 Craig, *Enemy at the Gates*, 124.

80 Ibid., 125.

81 McNeese, *Stalingrad*, 92.

82 Lesley Chamberlain, *Volga, Volga: A Journey Down Russia's Great River* (London: Picador Books, 1995), 141.

83 Ibid.

84 Ibid.

85 Ibid., 392.

86 McNeese, *Stalingrad*, 116.

CHAPTER 8:
A Trip Down the Volga

87 Hall, *Volga*, 93.

88 DeVilliers, *Down the Volga*, 303.

Auerbach, Loren, and Jacqueline Simpson. *Sagas of the Norsemen: Viking & German Myth.* London: Duncan Baird Publishers, 1997.

Berger, Melvin, and Gilda Berger. *Craftsmen, Traders, and Fearsome Raiders: The Real Vikings.* Washington, D.C.: National Geographic, 2003.

Chamberlain, Lesley. *Volga, Volga: A Journey Down Russia's Great River.* London: Picador Books, 1995.

Clarkson, Jesse D. *A History of Russia.* New York: Random House, 1961.

Craig, William. *Enemy at the Gates: The Battle for Stalingrad.* Old Saybrook, Conn.: Konecky & Konecky, 1973.

DeVilliers, Marq. *Down the Volga: A Journey through Mother Russia in a Time of Troubles.* New York: Viking Press, 1991.

Fairservis, Walter A. *Horsemen of the Steppes.* Cleveland, Ohio: The World Publishing Company, 1962.

Figes, Orlando. *Peasant Russia, Civil War: The Volga Countryside in Revolution (1917–1921).* London: Phoenix Press, 2001.

Florinsky, Michael T. *Russia: A History and Interpretation.* Vol. 1. New York: Macmillan Company, 1947.

———. *Russia: A History and Interpretation.* Vol. 2. New York: Macmillan Company, 1953.

Freeze, Gregory L., ed. *Russia, A History.* New York: Oxford University Press, 1997.

Graham-Campbell, James, ed. *Cultural Atlas of the Viking World.* New York: Facts on File, Inc., 1994.

Grant, Neil. *The Vikings.* New York: Oxford University Press, 1998.

Grey, Ian. *The Horizon History of Russia.* New York: American Heritage Publishing Co., 1970.

Hall, Elvajean. *The Volga: Lifeline of Russia.* Chicago, Ill.: Rand McNally & Company, 1965.

Halliday, E.M. *Russia in Revolution.* New York: American Heritage Publishing Co., 1967.

Jones, Gwyn. *A History of the Vikings.* New York: Oxford University Press, 1984.

Kirchner, Walther. *A History of Russia.* New York: Barnes & Noble, Inc., 1955.

Koch, Fred C., and Jacob Eichhorn. *The Volga Germans: In Russia and the Americas, from 1763 to the Present.* University Park, Pa.: The Pennsylvania State University Press, 1978.

Lamb, Harold. *The March of Muscovy: Ivan the Terrible and the Growth of the Russian Empire, 1400–1648.* Garden City, N.Y.: Doubleday & Company, Inc., 1948.

Magnusson, Magnus. *Vikings!* New York: E.P. Dutton, 1980.

Massie, Robert K. *Peter the Great: His Life and World.* New York: History Book Club, 1980.

Mazour, Anatole G. *Russia, Past and Present.* New York: D. Van Nostrand Company, 1951.

McNeese, Tim. *Stalingrad.* Philadelphia, Pa.: Chelsea House Publishers, 2003.

Moscow, Henry. *Russia under the Czars.* New York: American Heritage Publishing Co., 1962.

Riasanovsky, Nicholas V. *A History of Russia.* New York: Oxford University Press, 1963.

Rogers, Stillman D. *Russia.* New York: Children's Press, 2002.

Sawyer, Peter. *The Oxford Illustrated History of the Vikings.* New York: Oxford University Press, 1997.

Wallace, Robert. *Rise of Russia.* New York: Time-Life Books, 1967.

What Life Was Like When Longships Sailed: Vikings, A.D. 800–1100. Alexandria, Va.: Time-Life Books, 1998.

Wren, Melvin C. *Ancient Russia.* New York: The John Day Company, 1977.

Beevor, Antony. *Stalingrad: The Fateful Siege, 1942–43.* New York: Penguin, 1999.

Chamberlain, Lesley. *Volga, Volga: A Journey Down Russia's Great River.* London: Picador Books, 1995.

DeVilliers, Marq. *Down the Volga: A Journey through Mother Russia in a Time of Troubles.* New York: Viking, 1992.

Watson, Jane Werner. *Volga.* Silver Burdett Press, 1980.

WEBSITES

Volga River Information
http://acad.bryant.edu/~langlois/ecology/riversdraft.htm

Center of Global Environmental Education: Volga River
http://cgee.hamline.edu/rivers/Resources/river_profiles/Volga.html

The Volga River Basin
http://www.greencrossitalia.it/ita/acqua/wfp/volga_wfp_001.htm

The Siege of Stalingrad
http://history1900s.about.com/library/prm/blstalingrad1.htm

Image of the Volga River from Space
http://visibleearth.nasa.gov/cgi-bin/viewrecord?10294

Map and Information on the Volga River
http://www.volgawriter.com/VW%20Volga%20River.htm

INDEX

page:
3: Library of Congress,
LC-DIG-prokc-21216
7: Library of Congress,
LC-DIG-prokc-20023
13: © Mjeda/Art Resource, NY
17: © SEF/Art Resource, NY
26: © Bettmann/CORBIS
36: © Diego Lezama Orezzoli/
CORBIS
41: © Gregor Schmid/CORBIS
51: © Francoise de Mulder/CORBIS

60: © Bettmann/CORBIS
64: © Archivo Iconografico,
S.A./CORBIS
72: © Archivo Iconografico,
S.A./CORBIS
76: © Nik Wheeler/CORBIS
81: © CORBIS
85: © Bettmann/CORBIS
93: © CORBIS
97: © Wolfgang Kaehler/CORBIS
100: © Wolfgang Kaehler/CORBIS

Frontis: Courtesy NASA, *Visible Earth*
Cover: © Michel Setboun/CORBIS

ABOUT THE AUTHOR

TIM McNEESE is an Associate Professor of History at York College in York, Nebraska, where he is currently in his thirteenth year of instruction. Professor McNeese earned an Associate of Arts degree from York College, a Bachelor of Arts in history and political science from Harding University, and a Master of Arts in history from Southwest Missouri State University.

A prolific author of books for elementary, middle, high school, and college readers, McNeese has published more than 70 books and educational materials over the past 20 years, on everything from Indian mythology to the building of the Great Wall of China. His writing has earned him a citation in the library reference work, *Something about the Author*. His wife, Beverly, is an Assistant Professor of English at York College and the couple has two children, Noah and Summer. Readers are encouraged to contact Professor McNeese at tdmcneese@york.edu.